WILD ANIMALS AND THEIR WAYS

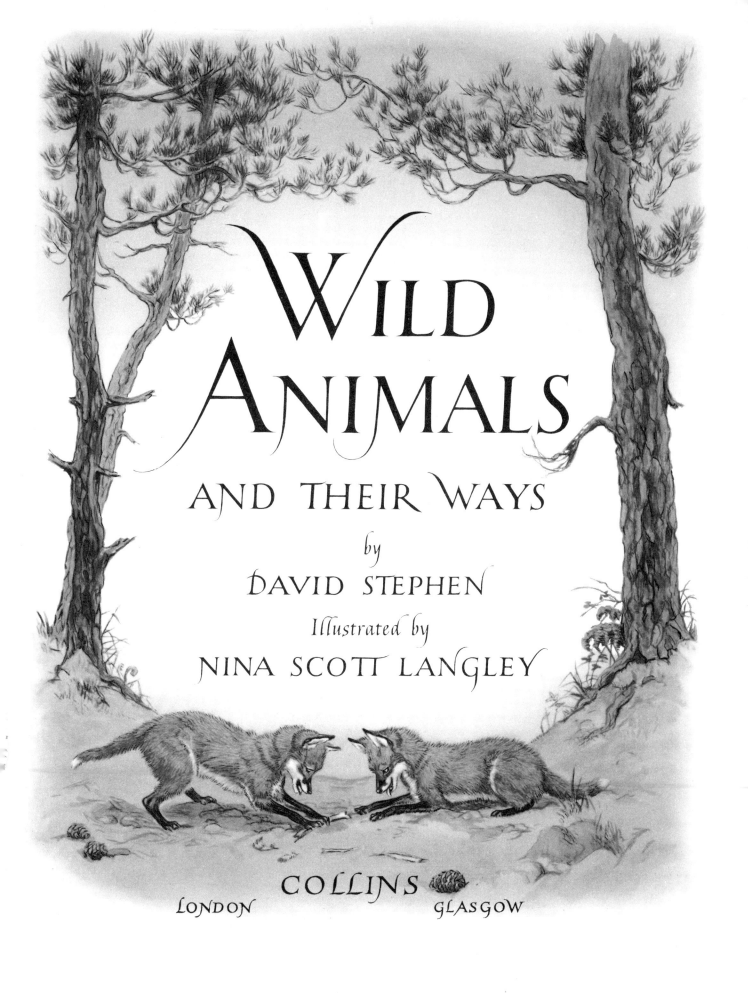

WILD ANIMALS
AND THEIR WAYS

by

David Stephen

Illustrated by

NINA SCOTT LANGLEY

COLLINS

LONDON   GLASGOW

For Fergus Ferguson
stalker, observer and good human being,
in gratitude.

—

Contents

The Fox

BRITISH foxes are a mixed lot, showing great variation in colour and size, with the biggest specimens coming, in the main, from Scotland. This has long been known, but it now seems that the difference in size is largely due to the fact that we have two types of fox. There has, however, been a great deal of importing and exporting, for the purpose of hunting—from Scotland to England, from the Continent to England, and from one part of England to another—so that big foxes or small foxes are liable to turn up almost anywhere.

This does not alter the fact that Scottish foxes tend to be bigger in the skull. leggier, and heavier, than the foxes of the English hunting counties.

Mention of the fox's name immediately brings to the minds of most people a picture of red coats, horses and hounds, misty mornings, bare trees and fields of stubble. That is largely an English picture; there are a few packs of foxhounds in Scotland, but England is the real fox-hunting country.

Hunting with hounds is a sport, and the fox has long been preserved for this purpose. Even to-day, when every man's hand is against the fox, riding to hounds is still a sport. Foxes are still overtly preserved in many areas, as they are still secretly imported into England from Scotland. The trade between Scotland and England isn't what it was, but it still goes on in a small way. Many masters of foxhounds will indignantly deny this, but I'm afraid it is perfectly true.

In the Lake District, where foxes are constantly harried because of their attacks on lambs, hounds are also used. But there the hunters follow on foot, and the hunt is more of a business and less of a sport. Nevertheless, there is a big element of sport attached to it, though it is a much tougher sport there than in the south.

In Scotland, except for the few areas where packs of hounds are maintained, the fox has long been treated as vermin, and fox-hunting is a different business altogether. There terriers take the place of foxhounds, and they are sent to ground at the very time of year when the foxes of England are left in peace, namely when the vixens have cubs.

In Scotland foxes are shot, trapped, snared and poisoned. Any way of destroying a fox is considered a good way, which is not in the best traditions of hunting in the Anglo-Saxon sense.

A sidelight on this is that, while England has abolished the gin-trap altogether, it will remain legal in Scotland for the purpose of taking foxes. But all the hunting and trapping and shooting has not seriously affected the over-all number of foxes anywhere. The fox we still have with us, and we are likely to have him for a long time to come.

The disappearance of the rabbit probably hurt foxes more than all the campaigns ever waged against him by man.

Why, considering that foxes kill rabbits, rats, voles and mice, does man wage such constant war against them? In the north of England, in the Southern Uplands and Highlands of Scotland, the fox kills lambs and sometimes attacks sheep, so he is hunted down at all times of the year. In all places he is liable to raid poultry houses, so the hand of every poultryman is against him, although it is a much easier matter to keep a fox away from hens than it is to keep him away from lambs. Then there are the game preservers: they wage war against the fox because he will, when he can, kill pheasants and partridges and grouse, and take their eggs during the nesting season.

Yet, despite this war, the fox contrives to keep going; keeping up his numbers whatever man may, or may not, do.

I have often asked people the question: what do you think foxes live on? And more often than not I have received the answer that they live on poultry, lambs, pheasants and rabbits. Yet this answer is, at one and the same time, only partly true and very wide of the mark. Lots of foxes go through life without ever killing a hen; more foxes die without tasting a pheasant than ever tasted one; and nobody knows how many foxes really kill how many lambs.

The fact is that the fox takes a great variety of food, pretty well indeed what he finds readiest to hand, and I have noted, at dens, the following items: blackcock, capercaillie, curlew, grouse, partridge, pheasant, poultry, peewit, roe fawn, leg of a red deer stag, hare, rabbit, rat, vole, fieldmouse, mole, frog and stoat. I have known foxes to catch squirrels, pull out the nest of a small bird from a bush, attack hedgehogs, dig up moles, and eat earthworms. They will also eat a variety of berries, and at a pinch will take vegetables, poultry mash and pellets, pig meal, and powdered milk. And, of course, they take lambs in the hill country, as everyone knows.

So you can see how dangerous it is to speak dogmatically about the fox's " usual prey ". The beast takes what he can get. And if he has a " usual prey " at all, that prey is far more likely to be voles, mice, rats and rabbits than anything else. And the rabbit is a comparatively recent item.

I have known a pair of foxes bring 63 rats to their cubs in ten days of hunting. I have known other foxes which killed mainly rabbits. I remember one pair that

10

dug out nine rabbit nests in and around the same wood, which probably meant that they had killed something like 50 baby rabbits.

Foxes kill moles but I'm not sure that they eat them; at least I have found a fox den at which several dead, and dried, moles had been used only as playthings by the cubs. At a pinch, however, a fox will eat a stoat.

When hunting, the fox will run a wall top, cross a frozen loch, swim, lie in ambush or even climb half-way up a tree. It has to be an easy tree, preferably one lying at an angle against another, or thickly bushed round the bottom; but climb he can. When hunted, even by one man and a dog, he will run through sheep (this I have seen a fox do), or in water, or on top of a wall, to hide his scent or take it off the ground. Whether he does this by thought, or without thinking, is a debatable point; but the result is the same. He has a strongly-smelling gland which tells the way of his going to any nose as good as his own.

The strong smell of the fox will assail your nostrils the moment you poke your face into the mouth of an occupied burrow. Some people can even smell a fox in the open under the right conditions. Yet the smell the fox carries about with him, which is not so strong when he isn't frightened or excited, doesn't affect in the least the working of his own shrewd nose.

Foxes, in severe weather, will try hard for poultry, and if one does get into a hen-house he will kill not only the hen he wants, but every other bird within reach. A properly locked hen-house is, however, proof against any fox, for the beast doesn't carry a key or a screw-driver.

Many a reynard finds easy prey by emptying snares; others will take rabbits from gins set in burrow mouths. A habit with others is to lie in potato drills waiting for pheasants coming along, head down, seeking creepy-crawlers or small uncovered potatoes. And there was one beast, near home, which snatched up a pheasant before my Labrador retriever could reach it. I remember another beast which lay among crowded moleheaps, looking like a moleheap himself, while partridges were scraping about twenty paces away. I am sure he was lying in wait for them.

Though foxes hunt late and early, and during the night, they do so quite readily by day where they are safe. I have seen them hunting late on in the morning at home and in the Highlands. But a Highland fox has to feel very safe before he'll do so. He knows what he is up against. That is why you won't find a hill vixen denning up in the kind of places often chosen by foxes in the hunting counties. She prefers the remote cairns, well out of man's way. For the same reason, Highland foxes are not so given to constant yapping. You'll hear more fox calls in a night in the south than you'll hear in the hills in a week.

Foxes pair at the beginning of the year, which is when they are most vocal.

11

Then you are most likely to see two running together, and, since the worst of the winter often comes at the same time, the pair will hunt as a couple. Indeed, in very hard winters, two pairs may hunt together on a single foray. It may simply be that two pairs run into each other when they're after the same thing. I doubt if four foxes would stick together for long.

I once watched four foxes trying to run down a small roe in deep snowdrifts, but I'm sure they weren't hunting as a pack. They were temporarily united from common interest. You get the same thing in the deer forests in severe winters when foxes discover a dead stag. As many as twelve foxes have been seen feeding on such a carcass at the same time. But this isn't packing; it is simply a matter of beasts using a common food supply in hard times. And in such a gathering there is constant bickering and fighting.

Dog fox and vixen running together are something else entirely. Then you get co-operation, a common purpose. I should think that, foxes being what they are, any association of more than two will be brief and unchancy. The calling of foxes is most readily heard in January and February. Dog and vixen both yap, but the vixen can also utter the most eldritch shrieks. Cubs are born in March and April. The vixen likes a ready-made den if she can find one, or she may enlarge a rabbit burrow. It isn't often that she will start from scratch, but I have known a vixen do it. In the Highlands rock holes are greatly favoured. So are the dens of mountain badgers, even when there are badgers in residence. But many vixens can't resist the easy digging

afforded by rabbit burrows, so that this kind of fox-den is to be found everywhere.

Many litters of cubs are born along our coasts, at the bottom of the inaccessible sea cliffs. I have known others born and reared in old mine workings, in whinstone quarries, and under a mere overhang of peat on open heather moor.

When fox cubs first begin to play at the den mouth they are droll little chaps, all fun and capers, with their heads full of fox-nonsense. They are playful as puppies; clinching, rolling, worrying and ragrowstering generally in the same way. At this stage they have a great deal to learn, and watching them isn't difficult if you can sit perfectly still with the wind blowing from the den towards you. Of course, a single warning bark from the vixen will send them bolting below ground, whether they know what it's about or not.

Many vixens, especially Highland ones, will let their cubs play by day in some secluded place away from the actual den. Others will take their cubs to the open heather and keep them there. This kind of playground is easily recognised. There was one near my home—on a flat above the burn—where a litter of cubs played every morning, and they had a maze of runways trodden through the tall growth of hogweed, meadowsweet, valerian and rushes which grew there.

Vixens are devoted mothers, and dog foxes are devoted fathers. Among our wild animals, fathers are not usually notable for their devotion to their families, but the dog fox is a noteworthy exception. He provides the food for his vixen and cubs, and continues to help his mate when she is out hunting herself. If his mate is killed he will rear the cubs if he can, and I have known several dog foxes who did so. If, of course, the cubs are very tiny when their mother is killed, so that they still require milk, there isn't much the dog fox can do about them. But if they are weaned, or near weaning, he will rear them.

Man and his dogs are the main enemies of foxes of any age, but cubs stand no chance against the hardy terriers used in the cairns of the Highlands. Sometimes, of course, there is an accident, so that fox and terrier die together below. There was one Highland terrier which was entombed in a hole for 32 days, after which it managed to get out. Probably it ate its way out through the body of the fox. One of my own terriers was buried for 11 days in a fox-hole before she managed to dig herself out.

Badgers can, and sometimes do, kill foxes which have moved in as uninvited lodgers, but I fancy most badgers put up with the nuisance without complaint. The most consistent enemy of the fox that I know of, man and his dogs apart, is the golden eagle. This great bird will carry off cub after cub until she has cleaned out the entire litter, and will attack an adult fox in the open. I have watched an eagle striking down at a big fox, but she didn't press home her attack. I have, however, seen many a fox cub carried to an eyrie in the talons of an eagle.

13

Fox cubs, like the young of most hunting animals, but probably more so than most, receive quite a lot of schooling. They learn to react at once to the warning bark of their parents. They are taught to use their noses when they are forced to find food which the vixen has deliberately hidden near the den. Sometimes they are given disabled prey so that they can try to kill it for themselves; more often they are given live prey in the form of young mice or such like, so that they can practise the art of pouncing and striking. Then, of course, there are the forays they make with their mother.

One doesn't often see a vixen out schooling her cubs, mainly, I suppose, because the foxes will be aware of the intruder before he knows about the foxes. I have been lucky enough to see a vixen with four cubs mousing in a hedgebottom; where her nose went their little noses went, and in this way they learned what to look for and where.

Cubs begin to leave home in late summer, and at this time one can sometimes see two cubs running together. But they soon part, for foxes are solitary beasts outside the breeding season. When they are at home the cubs usually have their own playthings; when they leave home they often carry their plaything with them. I remember meeting one cub who was carrying a tin by the saw-edged lid. Another I disturbed in a wood when he was carrying an old shoe!

Foxes, as I have already mentioned, vary a lot in colour. By and large, northern foxes are far greyer. There are others which are redlegs, which means they don't have the black stockings so common among English foxes in the south. Some animals have a white tip to their brush; others do not. But the presence or absence of the white tip is no indication of sex. There are white-tipped vixens and white-tipped dog foxes.

When the pupils of your eyes contract in the light they still remain round. The pupils of the fox contract into a vertical line like those of a cat. The fox's eyes are luminous at night when they catch the light, and may show green or crimson.

A fox, usually, is no match for a dog bigger than a terrier, and many a sheep-dog has killed a fox in the open. The strangest fight I have heard of was witnessed by a friend of mine in the Highlands. His sheepdog put up a fox on the hill, and fought with him. But the dog was very half-hearted about it; she appeared, rather, to be having a rough and tumble. The fox, however, was fighting hard, snapping and gripping the dog about the neck and face.

When the animals finally separated, the fox was shot. And it was then my friend noticed that the old fox hadn't a tooth left in his head! All he had were brown stumps, worn level with the gums.

14

The Badger

IT IS a good thing, when people start talking about the " cruelty " of flesh-eating animals, to remind them that the only animal who is deliberately cruel is Man. And you can cite the case of the badger.

Badger-baiting is illegal; it was a revolting sport, and no one with any feelings regrets that it has been outlawed. But it still goes on, as cock-fighting goes on, in quiet places, secretly. If you take a badger from his sett, put him in a sack, carry him to some open place, and spill him out for a gang of terriers to worry, that is an offence, because it is baiting. And no one pretends it doesn't go on at the present day.

If you take one live badger and put him in a barrel which is lying on its side, then send in one terrier after another to try and " draw " him out, that is baiting too, and illegal. But it goes on, up and down the country, more commonly in some parts than others. It is gross cruelty to the badger, and many a fine terrier is chopped and torn, often killed, to satisfy the " sporting " instinct of men who would try to tell you that wild animals are cruel.

And you must not think that this kind of thing happens only among people of so-called low mentality. It happens among " sportsmen " who pride themselves on their sporting behaviour. The late Mortimer Batten, who was a fine naturalist, tells the story of a Master of Foxhounds who slashed a tailed badger with his knife then threw the dreadfully wounded creature to foxhounds.

Let me explain a few of the relationships between men and badgers.

Highland foxhunters have often reason to be annoyed with old Brock, for they don't like to see their hardy little terriers maimed and cut up, and this is what often happens when fox and badger are in the same den. The alert foxhunter can usually tell when there's a badger at home, so he calls his dog off, or signals it out. Nevertheless many terriers are injured every year.

Yet, despite these accidents, most of the Highland stalkers and foxhunters I know, leave the badger alone. Others kill badgers as a matter of course, just as they kill foxes or eagles. But there are plenty of badgers on many forests, un-molested.

One day a keeper friend of mine was dogging a den for foxes. His terrier came

15

out after a bit, obviously scared. The keeper kept the dog beside him and presently a badger appeared and came right out, in daylight. The keeper kicked the badger on the seat and told him to be off! There must be few badgers who have been thus admonished.

The foxhunter in the south, who hunts foxes for sport, dislikes the badger for several reasons. When a terrier is put in a hole after a fox it may meet a badger instead, with dire results, which is exactly what happens in the Highlands too. But the southern foxhunter believes the badger kills a lot of fox cubs, which he thinks is an unforgivable thing, so he kills badgers, very often, as a matter of course.

Then Brock is such a digger! He is for ever burrowing, or opening up new holes, which makes the work of the earth-stopper more tedious. The badger, in short, is guilty of opening escape holes for the hunted fox! And that, as you can imagine, makes him very unpopular.

The poultryman has his doubts about the badger. So has the sheep farmer, and many shepherds believe that Brock is a killer of lambs. Poultry, lambs, fox

cubs—Brock is blamed, somewhere, at some time, by someone, for killing all three. What is the truth?

You must have noticed already how often the fox comes into any discussion about badgers. That is because they are frequently found together, sharing the same sett, and if you keep this fact in the back of your mind it will help you to understand a lot of things.

Take the alleged killing of large numbers of fox cubs. You may well ask why foxhunters, who claim to be helping to keep foxes in check, should object to badgers helping them in the work. The fact is they do. But do badgers really kill many fox cubs? The badger is a very clean animal; the fox is not. The fox is a dirty housekeeper, and clutters up the den with all kinds of smelly prey, so it wouldn't be surprising if the fussy badgers lost their tempers with their lodgers. Yet, though there is not the slightest doubt that a badger sometimes kills fox cubs, there is equally no doubt that most badgers simply resign themselves to their lodgers, and do not.

I knew one badger who not only killed the cubs of a fox; he killed the vixen too. But, if you think about it at all, you will realise that foxes would soon stop using badger setts if all badgers, or most badgers, were dangerous. The fox knows perfectly well that Brock is usually safe to live with.

Lamb-killing, if it can be proved, is a serious matter. I have never known, or heard of, a lamb-killing badger. Ernest Neal, who has studied badgers a great deal and whose book on this animal you should make a point of reading, has never found any evidence. The late Mortimer Batten, in his lifetime, had evidence of only one lamb killed by a badger. I have never met any naturalist, keeper or shepherd, who could swear to any badger killing a lamb. So you see the case for the badger is very strong. Which means that lamb-killing must be extremely rare indeed.

Poultry-killing is also a serious matter, and again one is faced with a great scarcity of evidence. It is probable that most badgers in most places never touch poultry at all. But in some parts of the country the evidence is beyond dispute. I have never known a badger to kill poultry, but I have heard of several cases on the most reliable evidence. On two occasions the badger was caught in the hen-house, in the act. It is a pity we do not know the age of the animals concerned, for I have a feeling they would be aged beasts.

I have noticed that reports of poultry-killing come from areas where badgers are very common, so that in the spring they may be short of food for a bit. But it is a fact that few poultry keepers, even in such areas, are ever troubled by a raiding brock.

Badgers take a great variety of food, both animal and vegetable, and from what I've seen of them I believe they prefer small prey to big. Brock is a fast mover

17

when he takes the notion—for a short burst he can be very fast indeed—but he usually reserves his sudden spurts for retreat. I have never seen one rush at anything, but I've seen more than one crash away at tremendous pace when scared.

Brock's hunting pace is a plod. He is bear-footed, and lumbers along bear-like. He can snatch, and turn, quickly, but he prefers to regulate his pace to the dictates of his nose. For this reason, big prey like hares or full-grown rabbits is beyond him, unless, of course, he comes across one trapped or snared, when he will squat and eat on the spot.

It would be true to say that he usually takes what is in front of his nose. Tiny leverets in their form are an easy prey for any hunter who stumbles on them. But they aren't easily found by mere searching, and I doubt if many are killed by badgers. Young rabbits are, however, another matter entirely.

The badger's way with rabbits in a nest is different from the fox's. The fox starts at the entrance to the nest and digs in, as a terrier would do, but the badger claws his way down from above. Once he has the young rabbits out he eats them on the spot.

Brock will kill, and eat, rats, mice and voles. Hedgehogs, which hunt when the badger is hunting, are sometimes caught and killed. The hedgehog isn't too fast for the plodding Brock, and must be one of the few animals he catches in the open by running it down. I imagine most of his animal food is found where it can't get away: young rabbits, rats and mice in their nests, older rats or rabbits in some hole, or perhaps in a trap.

A few years ago, in midwinter, I found badger tracks all over my back yard. They led to a heap of sand in the stackyard. The sand-heap was frozen hard, with a powdering of snow on top, and there were badger tracks all over it. The brock had been scraping at a small hole near the top of the heap. When I opened the heap with a pick my terrier dug in and killed eleven young rats in a paper nest. The badger had obviously been after them. I laid the young rats aside, and that night the brock came back and ate them all.

Badgers, I am sure, don't go looking for birds or their eggs, but they do stumble on ground nests from time to time. If they find eggs they will eat them. I doubt, however, if the average badger destroys many nests or nesting birds in his life. I have known a pheasant to get away with a brood of sixteen less than a hundred yards from an occupied badger sett. In one wood near home, the woodcock are never molested by the badger; they lose their eggs to the carrion crows. But I have no doubt that if a badger did stumble on such a nest, and managed to hold down the bird, he would kill it.

Far commoner foods than birds, eggs or hedgehogs, are slugs, earthworms and beetles. The badger, indeed, is a great hunter of insects. He will dig out the

18

nests of wasps and bumble bees, eating everything that is eatable. In some years, when wasps are rife, you will see the havoc wrought by badgers all over the place. During one night's foraging a badger must consume enormous quantities of grubs and insects of one kind or another.

Then there is vegetable food. Brock likes fruit. He will eat most wild berries, and in my area the doghip is a favourite in the late autumn. He is fond of acorns, very fond of the bulbs of the wild hyacinth, and eats a lot of grass when the berry harvest is over. You can, in fact, say that Brock is omnivorous.

My own badgers. which live at my home, will eat almost anything: hare, rabbit, horseflesh, cow-meat, mutton, eggs, milk, oatmeal and wheatmeal, dog biscuit, dehydrated meat, cooked maize, bulbs, tubers, potato, grain, tomatoes, sugar, mice and any kind of worm or insect I care to throw in.

It is commonly said that badgers won't eat carrion. They won't if we stick to the proper definition of carrion as putrefying flesh. But that doesn't mean the badger will not take anything that is already dead, or that has been dead for some little time. I have seen one feeding on a dead roe deer. They will take dead rabbit or rat so long as the carcass is reasonably fresh. But they won't take the putrid food the carrion crow revels in, and which the fox takes readily.

Brock is a true burrower. He is for ever digging, as the great mounds of earth outside the den show. And he keeps his den clean. He doesn't carry food in as the fox does, and leave the remains cluttering up the tunnels. He renews his bedding regularly, but the greatest activity is in spring and autumn. He has his latrines outside the den. And in remote areas he may have his sunning place.

Badger cubs are born in February and March, and begin to appear for short spells outside in April. At first they lack the wariness of their parents, and if you sit still beside a den the cubs will come almost among your feet—provided, of course, the old badger hasn't spotted you and sent the family rushing below.

Setts, however, are not occupied without a break. The den which had no badgers last week may have them this week, and the den which had them will be empty. There is a lot of chopping and changing. Not long after the cubs have begun to play about the den where they were born, they may be moved to another, but it isn't difficult to find them again.

If you sit down beside a sett during the day at this time you will often hear the thumps and rumbles of the cubs below, because their play becomes more and more boisterous as they grow. When they follow the old badger out at night they will rush and crash about, diving into one hole and out of another. Then they begin to dig holes of their own near the sett—holes which you'll find empty by day.

When an old badger comes out at night the first thing he often does is to have a good scratch. Then he will nose about before going off on his night's hunting. Runways radiate from the sett, and there is always one leading to water.

You have to be careful if you are waiting at a sett, because Brock has a wonderful nose. So you have to see that the wind favours you. If he gets a whiff of you he will dive into the sett and go rumbling away below. Sometimes a badger will come right out after only a few sniffs; at others he will stick his black-and-white face out a dozen times before he finally emerges.

From all this you will have gathered that badgers are nocturnal animals. In the main, they are. But I have seen badgers by day in March, June and July, and Highland badgers often live on the open hill after the cubs are able to get about. I have a friend who has three times put badgers on foot—a family of them—in the middle of the day in the month of June, out on the hill among thick bracken, far from any den.

Like fox cubs, young badgers have their playground, which they soon trample flat. It may be among bracken, or grass, or even among growing corn. I have several times seen such a trampled patch in a cornfield which adjoined a wood containing badgers.

Badgers do not hibernate in this country. It is true that, in the worst weather, they may not come out for nights at a time, but Brock is liable to behave like that at any time if he is well-fed or alarmed. A badger likes to gorge then sleep; he doesn't like to be out in a storm or during a period of lashing rain. But you'll find his tracks in the snow, even in the mountains, often at great heights. He is active in every month of the year.

Since they spend most of their lives underground, many badgers must die underground. What happens to them? Probably the other badgers in the sett dig a hole and wall the dead ones in. But Brian Vesey-Fitzgerald has observed badgers dragging out a dead member of the clan and burying the beast outside the den altogether.

From June onwards the badgers may be seen carrying in a lot of bedding, which may be grass from their own " hayfield," or bracken. Some beasts, in late autumn, take in bundles of fallen leaves. Bracken or grass is balled up, and trundled forward between chin and forepaws, but I have seen a badger moving backwards when the bundle was loose, as in the case of leaves. When old bedding is rolled out it is usually stuffed into a hole, or such place, near the den.

It must have occured to you, when looking at a picture of a badger, that his face is very boldly marked, whereas our other hunting animals are notable for the way their colour fades into their background. It has been said that the badger's black-and-white face matches the pattern of moonlight among trees. But I cannot say it has ever struck me like that. A badger's face is a strikingly obvious thing, from the moment it pokes from a sett on a dark night. Probably his face is meant to be obvious, as the skunk is obvious, and for the same reason. The badger is a powerful animal and fears nothing that roams the woods, except man himself.

There may be certain tricks of lighting that will render a badger invisible, or inconspicuous, but I have watched at setts on many a moonlit night and have never had any trouble seeing my badgers. Indeed, one tends to see more badgers than are really there.

SIZE: *Length 3 feet, of which 8 inches tail.*
WEIGHT: *Boar 25 pounds*⎫
            Sow 22 pounds⎭ *both up to 40 pounds or more.*
SEXES: *Alike. Female, Sow; Male, Boar.*

21

Pine Marten and Polecat

THE nineteenth century was probably the blackest in British history for the destruction of wild life. It was the heyday of the game-preservers, when every creature with flesh-eating teeth or a hooked beak, every creature which could, by any stretch of imagination, be considered a menace to game, was ruthlessly slaughtered. Anything that survived the nineteenth century slaughter was finished off, or nearly so, at the beginning of the twentieth.

Think of some of the names—names like pine marten, polecat, wildcat, golden eagle, sea eagle, kite, osprey, goshawk and peregrine—then consider just how likely you are to see such creatures to-day. The golden eagle you can see if you know where to look in Scotland, or an odd corner of Ireland. The peregrine we still have, in suitable places up and down the country, but the bird is still uncommon, and specially protected by law for that reason. The wildcat, after being nearly extinct by 1914, made a spectacular recovery and is now well established. But look at the others.

The polecat is extremely rare, with its last stronghold in Wales. The pine marten is rare, but coming back slowly in north-west Scotland. The goshawk has gone. The kite clings to life in a corner of Wales. The osprey is in a worse state, extinct as a breeder for years and fighting a losing battle to return. The sea eagle has gone.

A century ago pine martens could be killed in Scotland in hundreds. On Glengarry estate alone more than 100 polecats are recorded killed in three years from 1837 to 1840, not to mention 275 kites and 285 buzzards in the same period. Even although these figures may be stretched, as they probably are, the arithmetic is no less frightening. The pine marten, destroyed as " vermin," was prized for its pelt (it is a relative of the valuable sable) but you'd be hard pressed to make yourself a pair of gloves to-day from the skins of British martens.

If you read the literature of the period, you will find it both enlightening and depressing. Dr. MacDonald, in his book *Grouse Disease*, shows that almost every keeper and estate owner destroyed martens and polecats as a matter of course. Tom Speedy, who was the arch-priest of vermin killers, makes no bones about waging ruthless war.

23

Charles St. John was one of the greatest butchers ever let loose in Scotland. When he writes of martens he remarks on their bright dark eyes, describes the beauty of their fur, then tells you how he shot them. He shot every marten he could shoot, and when he wasn't shooting them he was cheering dogs on to worry them. St. John saw a lot of martens; he made sure we wouldn't be so fortunate to-day.

St. John was, nevertheless, an observant man. When most observers believed we had two species of marten—the pine and the beech—he was certain we had only one—the one we still have: the pine marten. He was right in his belief, for the beech marten was never a British animal. If he had been wrong at the time, he would probably have made himself right eventually by exterminating the beech marten, as he did the osprey in Sutherland.

Following the First World War the pine marten was in a very serious position. Its numbers were down to danger level, and it seemed that it must disappear altogether within a few years. In 1920, Dr. James Ritchie was drawing attention to this danger, but expressing the hope that the new forestry programme would help to save the remainder of our truly forest animals, of which the pine marten is one.

It looks as if this hope is to be realised. Great forests have been planted by the Forestry Commission since 1920, many of them within the marten's range, and there is no doubt that the beast is spreading out slowly. These forests provide thick cover for such species as the squirrel, woodpigeon and rabbit, all a menace to the forester or the farmer when there is no natural enemy to control them. The pine marten is such a natural enemy and, as such, will be welcome in the State Forests.

There is also the special conservation area at Kinlochewe in Wester Ross, where the marten is given sanctuary and where its habits are being studied by the scientific officers of Nature Conservancy. On the reserve it is thriving, but, unfortunately, many which leave the ground to take over new territory are either trapped or shot, for the marten has no protection in law.

It is doubly unfortunate for the marten that the gin trap has not been totally outlawed in Scotland as it has in England, for the beast is easily trapped, so will continue to be taken in gins as long as these can be legally set for foxes. Many people shoot martens on sight as they shoot any weasel-like animal, and the pine marten is a weasel. But, at the same time, there are numbers of enlightened landowners, with forests, anxious to help the species back to a safe level.

Despite its low numbers, the strange thing is that you have a better chance of seeing a marten to-day than fifty years ago, because the beast is quite regularly caught in car headlamps at night on the roads in the Kinlochewe area. A few have been killed in these circumstances; others have been shot not far away.

24

The marten is a great wanderer, and will therefore colonise new ground quickly if given the opportunity. That is why it is liable to turn up in forests far from Wester Ross, which is still its main stronghold. But trapping is the danger, and while most of this is perhaps accidental it is none the less serious. Jock MacRae of Sheildaig Farm, Gairloch, has taken a few in traps set for foxes, not because he wanted to but because the marten just never learns about traps.

Though I have said you stand a fair chance to-day of seeing a marten if you are in the right place, this is most likely to be in a trap or on a road at night. It is different when you go on the hill looking for the beast. You could spend weeks at Kinlochewe and never see one at all.

You may well wonder how the marten survived at all when most of the great Scottish forest was clear felled over the years. The fact is that the beast was driven to the hill where it took to living in cairns and screes and out-of-the-way corners. Like the red deer and the wildcat it became a haunter of the naked hill; like them its adaptability saved it from complete extinction, while the giant capercaillie, a forest grouse, disappeared completely.

The marten—often called sweet marten to distinguish it from the polecat—is about the size of a cat, but leaves a track like a hare, so that tracks are not a good indication of the beast's presence or absence unless you are very expert.

I had a salutary experience of this in the great snowstorm of early 1951, when I was motor-cycling in the West Highlands. The snow was deep; buzzards were down on the road feeding on dead rabbits; grouse were running ahead of me in dozens. I was approaching some scattered trees when the scolding of small birds attracted my attention, and there in one of the trees was a pine marten: a big, dark stoat with a great bushy tail. His throat and chest appeared white, but that would be a trick of the snow, for the marten's front is actually pale yellow.

I stopped the motor-bike and watched him leap from branch to branch with the agility of a squirrel, then he came down the tree backwards and raced to another tree with rump arched. I left the bike and followed him. When he left the second tree he bounded across the snow, up the hill and out of sight. He left tracks as like a hare's as could be without being a hare's.

The marten is really a forest animal forced to live on the bare mountains. In Scotland they will nest on the hill, among rocks, or in trees, in the old nests of crows, or squirrels' dreys. In Ireland old nests were frequently occupied. There may be martens left in Wales, as there are in the Lake District, but they must be very few. In the south of England there is a colony of pine martens, which belongs to H. G. Hurrell, who has written a great deal about them. Hurrell takes his martens into the woods where they play in the trees and follow him about; they return home almost invariably.

25

Hurrell says his martens will catch frogs; they like beetles and moths; and they pick blackberries and rowanberries. In the wild they take what they can get (a habit with predators generally): rabbits, squirrels, lizards, birds, frogs, fruit, wasps and honey. They can kill the fawns of the roe deer, which is about what you would expect with a weasel of this size.

By all accounts the marten is a fierce and brave fighter when cornered. When chased by dogs it will readily climb a tree, which is also a habit of the beech marten which I have seen in Europe. The pine marten can give a good account of himself against terriers in the open, and if found alive in a trap will fight back savagely. He is a beautiful, almost scentless weasel, but he is still a weasel.

26

Swift, agile, graceful, he is a match for any squirrel. On the ground he can go away at speed in bounds of over six feet, as I saw with the beast in the snow. Hurrell says his martens are not over-keen to go into a rabbit burrow; some do, others don't. Yet wild martens kill a great many rabbits, hunting by sight and smell, then going in with a final rush. Where rabbits were systematically trapped many martens were caught; the kind of fate which also befell the stoat.

When we come to the polecat—called foumart, foul marten, or fitchet, because of its disagreeable smell—we are faced with a great difficulty, that of telling the real polecat from the gone-wild polecat ferret.

The common white ferret is a domesticated albino polecat, but we also have the polecat ferret, which is very like the real polecat and which is able to survive and breed when it escapes to the woods. I find this kind of animal every other year, and have had one in my possession for a long time. It would not be considered a true polecat.

Yet these wrong-polecats, as I like to call them, are no different from the real thing. You can't tell by looking, and the anatomist can't even be sure in the laboratory. Polecat ferrets have always been going wild and wild polecats have

frequently been used for crossing with tame ferrets. So polecats are just as much mixed up as wildcats, and the wildcat is still a wildcat.

There are polecats on the Island of Mull which are the descendants of gone-wild ferrets, and are therefore not considered the real thing. But it seems to me that a polecat which looks like a polecat, acts like a polecat and breeds polecats which look like polecats, is a polecat for all practical purposes. You know that if a polecat raids your hen-house; right or wrong the result is the same.

So while no kind of polecat—right kind or wrong kind—could be called common, there are more polecats about than we are prepared to admit, or than we realise. I have put such a beast on foot, been snarled at, and left with a stink in my nose that no blue-blooded polecat could have bettered. And I have watched such a beast crouched over a pool, presumably waiting for fish, in the true manner of the real polecat.

Still, we must consider this great weasel, with the powerful musk glands, rare. But probably there are polecats in Scotland, the proper kind. There will be many more whose pedigree goes back to ferrets. The same thing will apply to England. But, whatever polecat you see anywhere, you won't know by looking whether it's the right or the wrong sort.

Wales is the real stronghold of the true polecat to-day, and the beast is even considered fairly common there, especially in the Tregaron bog area. It is mainly from Wales that accounts of polecat packs come to-day, for this species will run in packs as the stoat and weasel do.

The polecat has long been looked upon as vermin by game-preservers, and to a certain extent poultrymen, and it is true that once it comes into farming country it is liable to become a problem. It will kill far in excess of its needs, a habit it shares with the fox and the stoat. Rabbits were an important prey for this animal when they were plentiful, but it will take anything it can catch and hold. It takes eels, fish, frogs, snakes, game birds, eggs and poultry. It can kill a mountain hare, and the animal I had (the one of doubtful pedigree) caught and killed a big leveret.

A wounded polecat, or one which is being molested, will launch a gas attack from its stink-gland. This is powerful enough, but is not in the same class as the skunk's, for the polecat can't eject anything at the attacker. When trapped it will fight fiercely, and in certain circumstances will attack man.

As in the case of the rabbit, the gin trap accounted for great numbers of polecats. Where there were rabbit burrows, and trapping, polecats would be caught. In the same way, a polecat (of any kind) which is raiding a farm can generally be taken easily, because they have absolutely no trap sense.

Polecats will store food when they have young, in a chamber beside the nesting site, which may be a rabbit burrow, a hole in the rocks, a hollow tree, or some hole under a boulder.

Mortimer Batten tells of a polecat which could outrun his spaniel. He also describes the behaviour of an English polecat at Grimwith after he had shot at it. It " clucked and chattered, running broadside and bristling as a ferret does." It was the real polecat. And Wentworth Day tells of meeting one when he was a boy, in the fen country. What he remembers yet is the appalling smell the beast left behind when chased by a terrier: " the most appalling smell that ever smote the nostrils of man or boy in an English wood."

So our two big weasels, similar in many ways, differ as much as they possibly could in the matter of smell: the pine marten, faintly and agreeably musky, the polecat producing a real stench at will.

SIZE:	*Pine marten: Tail 12 inches; head and body up to 22 inches. Polecat: Tail under 7 inches. Head and body 14½ inches up to nearly a foot and a half.*
COLOUR:	*Pine marten: Thick, fine, sable fur. Tail thick and bushy. Throat and chest yellow in varying shades. Polecat: Long fur, almost black with purple sheen, but showing buff underfur. Light patches over eyes.*
BREEDING:	*Pine marten: Probably only once a year. Up to five kits. Polecat: Probably twice a year, 4 or 5 young.*
VOICE:	*Both species spit, hiss and chatter; and have a loud cry. The polecat's voice is said to be of deeper tone than the pine marten's, but this isn't any guide.*

Stoat and Weasel

THERE'S an old couplet of doggerel about the stoat and weasel which runs something like:

> The weasel's (w)easily recognised,
> But the stoat's (s)totally different.

This is true enough, but it doesn't tell us anything, so isn't of much use to us as a guide to identification.

Stoats and weasels are blood relatives, members of the same large family to which the pine marten, the polecat and the mink belong. They are the least of the weasels, in point of size, but not in any other way. Both are tireless, relentless hunters, often killing when they are no longer hungry, which isn't a bad thing (from our point of view) if the prey happens to be rats, voles, mice, rabbits and such like.

It is a great mistake to kill these animals as a policy, for both play an important role in preying on rodents. Unfortunately we keep on making this mistake. Stoats, for one reason and another, are not nearly so plentiful as they used to be, and I'm sure there aren't so many weasels about either.

The stoat is the larger of the two species, and a really big beast will run to fifteen inches, or even more, in length, and weigh up to 11 ounces. Much of the stoat's length is accounted for by his tail, which is over 4 inches, bushed like a squirrel's and tipped with black. Male stoats are bigger than females.

Apart from the mountain hare, the stoat is the only other British mammal which changes to white in winter, but the change does not take place all over the country, and white stoats are more common in some years than in others. In the south of England stoats may turn white, make only a partial change or no change at all. In Scotland the change to white is common, though I have seen specimens in the lowlands that made only a part change.

Probably there are more white stoats than we realise, for during long spells of snow, or even hoar frost, such animals are not easy to see. I have seen white stoats repeatedly during hard weather when the snow was lying for weeks at a time, but I have also seen them when there was no snow about and they were as easy to spot as a white cat on a green lawn.

Anyone who has watched stoats at all knows that they are both savage and playful; determined and relentless when hunting, and great ones for the capers in their spare time, so to speak.

A hunting stoat will bound forward like a rabbit; he will belly-crawl, wriggle, dart, weave and eel-twist; and he will sit up every now and again in listening attitude. Having acute hearing, his ears take second place only to his nose when he is hunting, and there are times when they guide his nose on to his prey in the first instance.

Though he hunts at night, the stoat isn't strict about it, and will be seen prowling by day, especially in hard weather. He will climb trees and corn stacks if his hunting demands it, and swim well when he has to, and if you happen to be

sitting on the bank where he wants to come ashore, come ashore there he will unless you actually keep pushing him off. I have had one dodging from side to side on a sandspit, trying to jink past me because he was not going back into the burn if he could help it. And jink past me he did in the end.

In the days when rabbits were plentiful, the stoat killed them in all sizes, outside and inside their burrows. You know how the rabbit behaves when pursued by a stoat: it crouches down, squealing, and gives up at once. We talk of such rabbits as " stoated " rabbits, and while I have no doubt most of them are " stoated " in the open from the moment the stoat marks them, the stoating begins for many of them in the burrow, from which they bolt when the enemy appears.

When he is on the line of a rabbit the stoat does not waste time running after every rabbit he passes on the way; he sticks to the one he has picked out, and it must be seldom indeed that he fails to catch up with it. Other rabbits, curiously enough, do not panic when they see a stoat running a line which isn't theirs.

Sometimes there is a kind of truce between stoats and rabbits, although I'm not sure truce is the right word. The fact is that when a stoat is living in a rabbit warren he will play about among, and with, his neighbours, who do not appear to fear him. I have watched half a dozen rabbits chasing after a stoat, then being playfully pursued by the stoat. It is equally certain that, when the stoat is hungry,

he will kill one of his neighbours. But there is this kind of truce at certain times.

A stoat will invade any burrow that he can get into, and I have watched a beast going into a rat-hole repeatedly. I have watched one climb a tree and kill a wood-pigeon on the nest, and I have seen one whisking along overhead rafters after rats.

Stoats breed only once a year, the young ones being born in early summer. The nest may be in a hollow tree, a hole in a wall, under a bank, in a rabbit burrow or a thicket, and it may be high up on a mountain. The female drags her prey to the nest to be eaten—she can haul prey two or three times her own weight—and I have watched one rolling grouse eggs through heather, and across a road, for more than a hundred yards. She rolled the eggs under her chin.

The stoat family sticks together as a unit for a long time, thus forming the well-known summer and autumn packs. Small winter packs may be no more than a single family, but large packs must be made up of two or more. These packs are probably formed when one family on the move meets up with others. I have seen a pack of seventeen hunting together, and I once became involved with such a party. I was bitten about the hands and face, but not seriously, for the stoat's teeth, though sharp, can't do a great deal of damage; the danger arises

from possible infection of the wounds. Attacking people is not, however, a common habit of the stoat.

But there is not the slightest doubt that other animals have a sensible respect for such packs. The fox will keep out of their way, and I have known one surrender his prey to a hunting party of stoats. Dogs which move in to kill often move out in panic. Such a party will attack harse (so, of course, will a single stoat) and invade the burrows made by grouse in deep snow. Stoats in this formation will, indeed, tackle anything they can catch and hold, even (in the words of W. D. Cocker) " unto big bubbley jocks," or geese. I have mentioned the stoat's prowess as a ratter, but I think the weasel is an even greater one. I also think it is a beast of more reckless courage. Imagine a little weasel, weighing less than a quarter of a pound, entering a barn swarming with big rats, and killing nearly a score of them before morning. I saw that happen many years ago at a farm in the Blane Valley in Stirlingshire. We shut the weasel in at night and counted the corpses in the morning.

A few years ago my wife and I watched a small weasel hunting the old wall behind the house. Three times in ten minutes we heard a rat squealing inside the wall, and twice the weasel came out dragging a dead rat. The little beast pushed and pulled and wrestled with each of them, moving them about ten yards to a pile of drain tiles, in which it hid them. That weasel was under 4 ounces in weight, I am sure; the rats were on the 16 ounce mark. I know, because we weighed them. And that isn't the biggest rat a weasel can kill; I have known one kill a rat weighing over a pound.

Weasels, being so tiny, can crawl into vole creeps and invade the tunnels of the mole. Voles are a favourite food with this species, but it kills a great variety of small mammals. It will take birds and their eggs, and will even tackle a hare.

Unlike the stoat, the weasel breeds twice in the year, roughly in spring and late summer. The young number four, five or six, and run with their mother for some time after they are weaned. Small family parties of weasels are not an uncommon sight in summer.

When hunting, the weasel sits upright from time to time in listening attitude, just as the stoat does. It darts about at incredible speed, but often bounds in the same fashion as the stoat. When a weasel is making its final rush on a rat or mouse it does so with its short tail stiffly erect, and the hairs on end. Perhaps all weasels do not behave like this, but I can't recall seeing one which didn't.

Female weasels are smaller than dog weasels, which is also true of the stoat, but in the weasel the difference in size is so striking that the females have often been taken for a different species. The belief is so strong in some places that the small beast has been given a different name: in Scotland the mouse-weasel. I believe the name in England is kine. But we have only one weasel, and the male happens to be much bigger than the female.

Weasels make their nest of grass or leaves in a hole in a wall or bank, in a tree stump or corn stack. They are much given to hunting on and in corn stacks, where they catch mice and sparrows.

They are great travellers, and no matter where you disturb them they seem to know every convenient hole in the neighbourhood. They spend as much of their hunting time below ground as above ground, and I have had a weasel emerge from a mole-run right between my feet. I have also seen a weasel in a corn stook, waiting for birds to alight.

Both stoat and weasel are extremely curious, which is often the death of them. If you disturb either, and the beast seeks refuge in a wall or bank, it will come out soon if you stand by and wait. In the same way they will return time after time to prey, even when you are standing a few feet away. And it is a fact that if one of a family is killed, say on a road, the others will come out to drag the body away. You can understand how habits like these make the beasts an easy prey for the man with a gun.

In this country, the weasel does not change to white in winter. The winter coat is, however, paler than that of summer. The beast is smaller than the stoat in every way: shorter in the body and legs, with a smaller head, and a short tag of a tail untipped with black.

SIZE: *Stoat:*   *13 to 16 inches, of which tail over 4 inches.*
                          Weasel: 7 to 11 inches, of which tail about 2 inches.
WEIGHTS: *Stoat:*   *From 4 to 11 ounces.*
                          Weasel: From 2 to 4 ounces.
BREEDING: *Stoat:*   *One litter; up to 8, sometimes more.*
                          Weasel: Two litters of 4 to 6.

The Otter

THE otter is the sleek weasel of the water, another member of the great, persecuted *Mustela* family: a night hunter, rarely seen by day unless put on foot by dogs, difficult to watch at any time. His " crime " is eating fish. . . .

Anglers, by the very nature of their sport, see more of otters than most people —not hunted otters, but otters going about their proper business of living. Most knowledgeable anglers to-day have no quarrel with him. Fishery Boards take him for granted, for the most part. Many river owners accept him as part of the scene. Some believe he is an asset on a river, which I believe is correct.

Then, recently, there was the report to the Otter Committee, prepared by Marie Stephens, which has brought to light much new material, and in no way justifies routine destruction of otters. This is a very fine report, which you ought to read.

But observations and research apart, there is one thing that can safely be kept in mind. We have had fish and otters for thousands of years; we still have them. Any decline in river fishing is not due to otters. On a fish farm the beast can be a menace; on his ancestral rivers he is just one of the ancient citizens, behaving as he was meant to behave. And no part of his job is to eat himself out of existence.

Every movement of the otter is beautiful to see; his every pose is one of grace. In the water his action is noiseless, sinuous, without press of bone or bulge of muscle; on land, his gait is the rump-up, bounding run of the true weasels.

One of my most vivid recollections is of an otter stalking ducks on a frozen loch, on a night of intense cold and brilliant moonlight, during the calling season of foxes in the savage winter of 1946–47.

I was numb with the cold, and ready to leave for home, when I saw the otter against the frozen snow on the steep bank away to my right. He sat there for some time, a smudge against the moon-washed snow, and I could imagine him trying to figure out how he was going to get near those ducks. He managed it by running round the shore—hump-backed, in true stoat style—through sere reeds and peaty hummocks, then working up on the birds in the shadow of the bank. A quick rush would take him among the nearest of them.

His attack was swift and perfectly timed, and he was in among the dozing

birds before they realised what was happening. There was a wild swish and whistle of wings, and much quacking, as the startled birds swung into the air; but one lay dead at the otter's feet while the others trailed in ragged procession across the face of the moon. Not long after that a fine 22-pound dog otter was shot on a burn just over a mile away, and I wondered if he was the beast I had watched that night.

I doubt if otters catch many ducks, but moorhens are a common enough prey. When the water is open the otter swims under the birds and pulls them down by the leg; on ice he stalks them. In very hard weather an otter may raid a poultry house. But if there are rabbits where he is hunting he will take these more readily than anything. Otters passing through my neighbourhood take a lot of rabbits, and I have found their tracks beside the remains of a moorhen.

It is as a fisherman, however, that the otter is in his proper rôle, whether the prey is eels, coarse fish, frogs or game fish. There is no doubt that he kills great quantities of eels, and that he likes frogs. There is equally no doubt that he takes salmon and trout. He has been doing all these things for a very long time: long before men began to record his doings. Salmon are menaced by man and his works as they can never be by otters.

Naturally, the otter's food varies somewhat from place to place. He takes what he can find, and frogs and eels bulk large in his diet. He also takes carrion. But he has his basic needs, and rivers which can't support him in the way of fish will seldom attract him no matter how many rabbits or other things there may be at hand.

An exception to this was the bitch otter who had two cubs less than 400 yards from my house in the spring a few years ago. There's a lot of small trout in the burn, and at that time the place teemed with rabbits. But I wouldn't have thought the place would attract an otter. I was wrong. Travelling otters often follow the burn, but I had never known of one breeding there. I watched the bitch and cubs many times in the early morning and evening, until they left.

In late March, another year, I watched a bitch with one cub catching frogs in an old quarry pond. The cub was big, so must have been a winter one. The beasts caught frogs by pushing their heads under the shallow water, and ate a

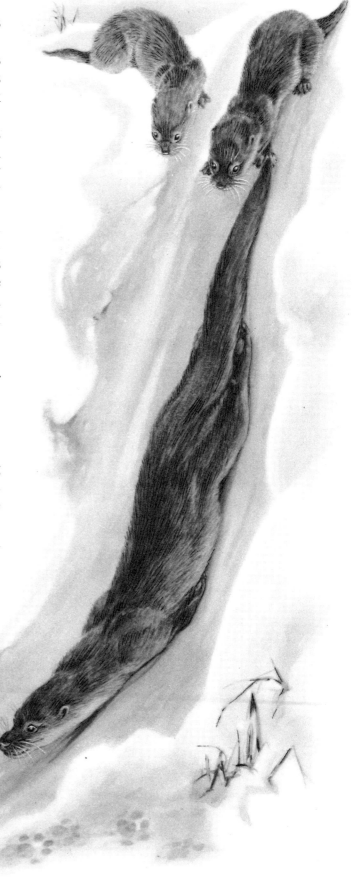

number of them. The pond was dirty, so that the otters were plastered with mud, but a short swim, and a little work with their tongues, soon cleaned their fur, and they left for the glen. I never saw them again.

On the coast, and in such places as the Outer Hebrides, the otters use holes in the rocks, or small caves, often difficult of access. The otters of the outer isles spend most of their time by the sea, but are not sea-otters. They eat a lot of crabs and shell-fish, and probably do not travel far from their birthplace—perhaps no farther than the length of the short rivers. Highland otters, on the other hand, are great wanderers, and will travel many miles over the high ground. I have seen otter tracks going right over a ridge at 1,200 feet.

The most settled time for otters is the breeding season, for the bitch will not move on until her cubs are swimming strongly and catching their own fish. Dog otters usually lie downstream from their mates, and will fight any other dog otter who tries to move past them. Just what part the dog otter takes in the rearing of his family is still a matter of argument. It is unlikely he sees the cubs till they are in the water. After that he may play with them and catch fish for them.

Otter cubs may be born in any month. This has long been suspected, and many people were sure of it. The investigations of the Otter Committee support this. As I have said, I have seen a well-grown cub in late March and others no bigger in June. But there may be some variation between one district and another.

Autumn is the time of movement, and otters begin to move up-river in the wake of the running salmon. I see this movement almost every autumn at home, where most of our otters are travellers, and I have watched a beast far out on a heather moor, many miles from the next river. During this travelling period a beast will often lie up for several days in a place where food is plentiful.

Otters moving overland, as these beasts do, often run into serious trouble. They may be taken in traps set for rabbits or foxes. And they are sometimes harassed by dogs. A big otter fears no single dog, and will fight fiercely. One beast, set on by two greyhounds, gave the dogs a mauling, and was still fighting gamely when the owner of the dogs killed him with a hatchet. He was a fine beast, scaling over 23 pounds.

A strange thing about otter cubs is that they do not willingly take to the water. They have to be coaxed in or pushed in, and it is some little time before they become expert at catching their food. I doubt, however, if they have to be "taught" to swim. Once they are in the water they have either to swim or drown. They swim. A bitch otter with cubs in the water is a delightful sight, and it is here that the angler, going quietly about his sport, often scores over the active seeker.

Besides the Otter Report which I have mentioned, I recommend to you, for reading, *The Wandering Otter* by H. Mortimer Batten.

The Wildcat

THE true wildcat is found to-day only in the Scottish Highlands. All over the country you'll come across cats running wild, and they are wild enough in habits and temperament; but they are impostors.

All sorts of cats turn up in the woods and on the hill, living the free life. There is the poaching domestic cat, hunting free but still attached to somebody's house. There is the domestic cat, born on the hill but of pure domestic parents, which has never seen the inside of a house and is wild enough by any standard. Then there is the half-bred cat—the offspring of a wild tom and a domestic tabby—which is big, fierce and powerful, and half-way to being a real wildcat.

The genuine Scottish wildcat is a magnificent beast, a miniature tiger—wide-skulled, flat-eared, with blunt, bushy tail clearly ringed. A

good tom will scale up to 15 pounds and measure well over three feet from tip to tip; beside him the domestic tom is a sleek, slim, whiptail. The wildcat is longer in the leg and longer in the teeth, infinitely more powerful, fit indeed to argue with any fox which the domestic cat is not.

Intractable and untameable: such is the wildcat. Most of them do not take kindly to captivity; others have lived for many years in cages. But the caged wildcat is as savage at the end of his days as he was when taken from the hill as a kit. Even the half-bred is a morose, highly-strung spitfire. It took me seven weeks, with constant handling, petting and feeding, to win over a kitten taken at 6 weeks old. But it could never be trusted with strangers.

Fifty years ago, when game preservation was at its peak, the wildcat was ruthlessly thinned out, its remnants being hemmed in north of the Great Glen and in the wild mountains of the west. There it was driven to seek its strongholds in the high corries and cairns, in rocky fastness and steep screes; on the sheep-runs and grouse moors it was shot and trapped almost out of existence. And no animal is easier to trap.

To-day, however, the wildcat is probably as numerous as it has been at any time within living memory. It is found far south and east of the Great Glen, and the new forests have afforded it sanctuary.

A half-bred cat is a clawing, bristling fury, and I have been bitten by one clean through a thick glove; my wife has a scar on her chest to this day, the result of a claw-stroke through thin clothing. A real wildcat is far more powerful, a beast of indomitable courage when at bay, and a female with kits in the heather will face almost anything in their defence. Wildcats bolt readily to terriers, so it is never a wise thing to kneel down and peer into a hole. A Perthshire shepherd did so and a spitting bundle of barbed-wire hit him right in the face.

But you must not think that the wildcat is a beast which will make an un-provoked attack on man. It will make room for him every time, although it may do so with a great display of fireworks, as indeed a half-bred cat will too. I have never stumbled on a wildcat with kits in the open, but I fancy such a situation might be unpredictable. I have, however, put up an adult in the open, and was treated to much hissing and spitting before the beast disappeared among the rocks.

One June morning, about half-past four, I was on my last lap to an eagle's eyrie when I met a wildcat among the rocks. She grimaced and spat as I walked below her, bristled flat-eared when I was within twenty paces, then turned away and vanished among the rocks. I searched among the boulders for more than half an hour, without meeting up with her again or seeing any sign of kits. Yet kits she did have, for I saw one of them nearly a fortnight later.

The eagle's haunt is the haunt of the wildcat, and I have been luckiest with

44

wildcats when I was photographing eagles and spending night after night out on the hill. In spring and late summer, the cries of the wildcats can be heard at night. One night on a hill in Perthshire I was kept awake for several hours by the dismal chorus of wails and shrieks of a pair of cats; towards morning we heard the terrible caterwauling just outside our small tent.

Wildcats trap easily, and a trap set in the same place will take beast after beast. A trap set on a tree across a burn is a favourite practice with keepers and shepherds, the cat either drowning or dangling until someone comes along to knock it on the head. Traps set at dens are sure to be sprung eventually.

Wild kittens are born in spring and early autumn. The European wildcat breeds only once, but the Scottish race does so twice, perhaps three times in some cases, which indicates the presence of domestic blood in our animals. Kittens can be found in early summer and autumn, and that seems to clinch the matter.

Probably the wild tom takes no share in providing for his family. I should think it unlikely, but it is dangerous to lay down the law where wild animals are concerned, and the behaviour of domestic tom cats should not be taken as a certain guide to the behaviour of wild toms.

Two to four kits seem to be usual, and the youngsters, once they are able to run about, follow their mother about, as the kittens of the domestic cat do.

Wildcats eat raw, fresh food. They do not eat carrion, or food that is tainted. A half-bred cat will do well on horseflesh, but Mortimer Batten, who knew a lot about wildcats, was quite definite that this was not suitable for them. He named pigeons and sparrows as other dangerous foods, though it is difficult to see why this should be so.

When rabbits were plentiful, the wildcat killed them in large numbers, and there is no doubt they were a favourite food. But voles and mice are also common prey. Squirrels are taken—I have seen a wildcat kill a squirrel, and know a domestic tom which can catch them at any time—and cats in the forests must kill many of them. The mountain hare is also preyed on. And the wildcat is fit to tackle the fawn of the roe deer. Any bird that the cat can catch and hold will be taken.

I often wonder just how many roe fawns or red deer calves are killed by wildcats. A year or two ago I watched a group of hinds in Ardgour, moving in among rocks in a body and driving a wildcat up to the heights. Roe does and red deer hinds are watchful mothers, likely to deal out summary punishment to any cat that attacks their young.

Wildcats are blamed for killing a lot of lambs, which is why shepherds wage such war against them. But lamb-killing is a thorny problem, and it is extremely difficult to get accurate evidence about the numbers killed by cats.

46

The wildcat will eat fresh fish, but fish isn't thought to be a prey the beast cares much for. They do, however, eat it, and will hook stunned or injured fish from the water. The Marques de Torrehermosa told me of a wildcat which was found drowned in a fish-trap, so that one at least was after fish.

Sight is probably the sense the wildcat uses most when hunting. He will listen, and smell, but he does much of his stalking by sight. Once he is within range of his quarry he goes in with a rush, and he is very fast in a short burst, as I saw with the cat I watched catching the squirrel. Prey is usually dragged into some kind of cover—rocks or brushwood or heather—and eaten there. Like other hill beasts, the cats come down in hard weather, but I have tracked them in deep snow over 1,500 feet; under normal conditions they will hunt right to the tops.

Apart from man and his dogs, the wildcat has few active enemies. If he harasses deer calves he may find himself being trodden underfoot, but that is his own doing. The golden eagle may take a kitten once in a long time. But man is the only serious, active enemy, and more wildcats die by trap and gunshot than by any other means.

Squirrels

THE red squirrel is our native species; the grey is an alien. Most Scottish red squirrels to-day are probably of English extraction; all greys are American.

It is thought that the felling of the Scottish forests last century virtually exterminated the red squirrel, except in a few areas like Rothiemurchus and Strathspey. It is a matter of history that Scandinavian squirrels were brought in by the Duke of Atholl in 1790. But other parts of the Highlands, and Lowlands, were stocked with English reds.

You might think that bringing English red squirrels to Scotland was no different from bringing American greys to Britain. But there is a world of difference. English squirrels turned down in Scotland were being released in a country of which their kind was a native, and came from another part of the same island. The grey was never a native, and came from across the Atlantic.

The spread of the grey squirrel is an object lesson on the danger of introducing foreign animals. We all know about the disastrous result of the rabbit's introduction to Australia. The grey squirrel has become so numerous here, and is such a pest, that the Forestry Commission was paying a bounty for tails until 1958; yet a century ago people were actively encouraging the little beast because he looked so charming.

The first liberations of grey squirrels took place in the south of England. They were introduced to one part of the country from another. And the Americans showed that they were real pioneers and hustlers. They spread rapidly on their own initiative, and were always being assisted by misguided people.

Hardy and adaptable, the grey squirrel will colonise suitable ground anywhere. He will travel over miles of open country to invade new woods. Now he has become established in Scotland, where he was deliberately introduced, and is in strength in many parts. I have found greys often in places where they were not supposed to be at all, many miles from the nearest colony.

It was once thought that wherever the grey squirrel went he killed off the red, and certainly the grey did build up his numbers in the very places where reds were dwindling. It also seems true that the red finds difficulty in recovering ground held in strength by greys. But squirrels, like other animals, have their ups and downs. The red squirrel is notable in this respect, and it seems that he was in a decline anyway when the grey squirrel's wave of invasion took place. So the grey was taking over ground from which the red was already disappearing, and probably completed the process by sheer weight of numbers.

From time to time there are reports of grey and red squirrels interbreeding, just as there are of rabbits and rats. But there has never been any proof of cross-breeding. Grey squirrels with ruddy necks and shoulders are pure-bred Americans.

We have the grey squirrel so much with us now, and he has been so much publicised, that we tend to forget that our red squirrel could be a pest too, and was quite a serious one in some forests. Both species bark trees, the greys concentrating on hardwoods and the reds on conifers. But the greys have been damaging conifers, too, as the Forestry Commission knows, and both attack the leading shoots of larch, pine and spruce, which causes distortion and flat tops.

At the present moment, however, the red squirrel is not dense enough in most forests to do serious damage. The day may come when it will be. And then the pine marten, if it is present again in numbers, will come into its own, for this weasel of the trees is the great natural enemy of the squirrel, and was probably the main controlling force in the days of the great Caledonian Forest.

Red squirrels will take fruit of all kinds, as well as cones, beech-mast and acorns. They also eat a variety of greenstuff, hips and other berries, twigs, buds, fungi, ants' eggs, birds' eggs and, in some cases, nestlings. I have seen a red squirrel eating nestlings on the ground.

The time of great bustle for the red squirrel is in early autumn: harvest time. Then you will see him gathering and burying; or gathering, carrying and burying. In this way he plants hazel nuts, acorns and beech-mast, thus planting trees, for I am sure he forgets more than half his hiding places.

In 1957 I spent more than a week watching red squirrels feeding on a forest edge, where there was a heavy ground carpet of leaf mould. I laid out little heaps of bait, including nut-and-raisin chocolate, and watched the squirrels burying these. Later I filmed one of the two animals concerned, scraping the titbits up again, and eating them.

The burying habit is at its height, however, in autumn, and sometimes an animal will lay up a considerable store in one place, as the stoat will do and the wood-mouse will do. I have found a store of beech-mast in an old nest. Near home, in a year of good acorn harvest, I saw a squirrel carrying acorns to a hole in a big tree. Squirrels had only recently been turned down on that estate, and were, indeed, being fed with hazel nuts laid out on trays. Every squirrel-box contained a good store of these nuts.

The nest of the squirrel is called a drey, is made of twigs and built in a tree. Leaves and moss are built into the structure, which is a ball with hardly any visible entrance. Bits of bark or moss or twigs lying at the bottom of the tree show that a squirrel has been working, just as wood chips betray the woodpecker.

Monica Shorten, in her very fine book on *Squirrels*, says that the red squirrel in England may produce two litters in a season, but that one is the rule in Scotland. I do not know about England but one litter is almost certainly correct for Scotland. I have found helpless young in May, and not later, and any youngsters seen in the trees later on looked what I would have expected May-born youngsters to look like.

Squirrels do not hibernate, but will lie up during storms. They have to eat often, and day after day, in Atholl, I have watched the red squirrels in the larches when there was deep, frozen snow on the ground, with the sun shining. The squirrel can trim down a larch cone until it looks like a cigar, with a small tuft at the end.

Man is the squirrel's most serious enemy to-day, because he can organise destruction. Some terriers can catch squirrels. There is a cat I know, belonging to a stalker friend of mine (or, rather, to his wife) which seems to be able to catch squirrels as it pleases. But the wildcat is a good squirrel hunter, so one would expect a big domestic cat to be fair. Then, of course, there is the marten, the great squirrel killer.

I am not sure that many foxes kill squirrels although some certainly do. I have watched a red squirrel make a fool of a fox, and any squirrel will scold any reynard he sees. When feeding, the red squirrel is watchful, and likes a prominent place to eat on. Once, during the leaf-fall, I watched one on a bird table. Every time a big sycamore leaf came down, casting its shadow on the table, the squirrel leaped to the ground and behind a tree. This suggested to me that squirrels may expect attack from the air.

51

Red Deer

IT IS June in the Scottish Highlands: the unpredictable month of torrid heat, snell winds, lashing rain and freak storms. Eagle and peregrine falcon have young in their eyries; the year's broods of ravens, glossy and blue-black, are on the wing; wheatears and ring ouzels are carrying food to their chicks.

Everywhere, scattered along the hillsides, from the glens to the high ridges, graze Highland blackface ewes, with fat lambs at foot. . . .

For the red deer hinds it is an important time. Now they slip quietly away from the main herd to give birth to their spotted calves. Though the country is vast—a wild country of mountains, and lonely glens, and stupendous screes—the deer are way-wise, and know exactly the spot where they want to be at this time.

Red deer calves are small things—specks in the vastness; yet they are not difficult to find if one watches closely the shy, cunning, secretive hinds.

Over yonder, across the glen, five hinds are grazing, on the roughly terraced slope in the shadow of the eagles' crag. They are alert, on edge, forever throwing up their heads, to stand with nostrils flared and ears swivelling, seeking hint of danger. They have calves hidden somewhere near at hand.

If we watch long enough we'll see first one hind, then another, moving away from the group. Presently she will put up her calf and nurse him. After a spell she will nuzzle him down again. So all we have to do is make a note of the spot, then cross the glen to make his closer acquaintance.

You don't have to wait for the hind to give her calf away, but it is the surest method. You can move on to where the hinds are grazing, and simply cast about in the likeliest places until you find a calf or calves. The hinds will run off at your approach; but they won't run far. And they'll halt where they can get a view, and watch you all the time you are near their calves.

Hinds have their favourite calving places, and it is more than likely that you'll find beasts in the same place year after year.

When you come on a calf you'll be struck by the fact that it lies perfectly still, even when you touch it. Its only movements will be the involuntary kind—the heave of flanks while breathing and the occasional flicker of an eyelid. This lying still may be the price of survival, and the calf plays the game according to the rules.

You may have heard that if you touch a calf, leaving your scent on him, his mother will desert him or even kill him. This is quite untrue. Hinds are devoted to their calves, and man-smell doesn't change their nature. Indeed, the hind will move her calf to a safer place, and the next time you come across him he'll know what you are, and run away if he can. I have handled five calves in a row, then watched the hinds come back and move them to new quarters. There was no question of desertion. The Nature Conservancy's field zoologists on the island of Rum are ear-tagging a lot of calves for research purposes: this they could not do if every other calf they handled was afterwards deserted by the hind. I asked these field workers about desertions by hinds and they had never known of a single case.

It must not be thought that a hind, because she leaves her calf by himself for hours at a time, is being neglectful. She has to eat, and it takes time for her to graze her fill. Her calf, until he is strong enough to run with her, is safer out of sight, where she can keep track of him. So she leaves him down. But at the slightest threat of danger she will return to him to defend him, against anything except man.

Eagles and foxes are potential dangers to a calf, but I doubt if either kills as many as we like to think. Once in a while, a calf will be found at a fox den or in an eagle's eyrie, but the only calves I have found in an eyrie were already dead when they were picked up.

A red deer hind is an able beast. If a fox comes too near her young she will drive him off, dabbing with her forehooves. She will do the same thing with a wildcat. And a hind isn't likely to stand by and watch an eagle kill her calf. She is far more likely to stand close to him, and rear up, striking the air with her hooves, to drive the bird away.

A hind who gives birth to a dead calf will stay with him for perhaps a couple of days, reluctant to part from him. I remember one such beast. On the second day she left at last, and then the eagle moved down to take possession of the body. I doubt if nursing hinds have any real fear of eagles, or that they really consider the birds a menace, for I have found calves on many occasions born close to an occupied eyrie.

When the calves are up on their legs, they follow their mothers to join the hind group, and it is a pretty sight to see such a herd of hinds and their followers —little spotted calves, yearlings, and older animals.

A stag calf, in good condition, will begin growing his antlers when he is a year old. While this single spike is growing it is covered in velvet, which is warm and furry, and supplied with a network of fine blood vessels. This velvet begins to peel in July or August, and the young beast rubs it off. When the antlers are clear of velvet they are said to be clean. The young stag cleans his first antlers when he is about 16 months old.

This is the head he will carry until the following spring. Then he will cast his spikes, and begin to grow new antlers: his second head. These antlers will, as before, be in velvet during the growing period, and will be cleaned in autumn. The following spring they will be cast, and this pattern of casting, growing, and cleaning the stag will follow throughout his life.

The beast who cleans his first spikes in his second autumn (when he is called, in Scotland, a knobber) may grow to be a great Royal; he may turn out an indifferent stag, fit to be classed only as a " rag " or " rubbish " by the stalkers; or he may become a switch—a beast with no points above his brow-forks.

Stags, after they have grown up, are known by the number of points, or tines, on their antlers: thus 6-pointer, 8-pointer and so on. A Royal is a stag with 12 points, six on each antler: brow, bay, tray, and 3-point top. If he grows more than twelve points he becomes known as an Imperial.

Feeding has a lot to do with the quality of a stag's antlers, which is why park stags can produce such great heads. Fine heads are also to be seen in Germany. Scottish hill stags rarely show much beyond the Royal stage, and not so many become Royals.

It used to be thought that deer lived to a great age, but the fact of the matter is that they are old before boys become men. Once a stag has produced his best head, he begins to go back, which means that his antlers deteriorate with advancing years. Hornless stags, known as hummels in Scotland, are beasts which have never grown antlers; age for age they are usually heavier than antlered stags.

Except at certain times of year red deer tend to herd by sex; thus you find stag herds and hind herds. But you will find the knobbers and young staggies running with the hinds. On ground where both sexes spend the year you will find all kinds of mixtures, but the main groups stay apart for most of the year. In other forests only hinds will be found in certain areas (hind ground) and stags in others (stag ground).

It isn't uncommon to find two or three big stags accompanied by a young staggie, or even a knobber. The young beast stands guard for the old stags, and is the one to watch carefully if you are trying to get close to such a group.

Any time after mid-September the rut begins. This is the mating season, when the stags grow manes, find their voices, wallow in the peat, and rip heather with their antlers. The leonine roaring of the big stags is confined to the period of the rut; at other times they use their voices little, though I have heard a hummel roaring in June.

When the rut breaks the stags burst in among the hinds, each taking over a harem. On forests where there are groups of both sexes the stags don't have to travel far, but some stags travel great distances to reach the hinds. For example, big stags from the forest of Black Mount will cross clear to the head of Loch Rannoch in search of hinds.

A master stag in possession of hinds roars, grunts and snorts, and sometimes appears almost to be sobbing. He is kept constantly on the move by younger stags waiting nearby, ready to move in and run off some of his hinds. He is given little opportunity for sleeping or eating. He is forever alert. He is the master, but his mastership is temporary.

55

Thus, for ten days, a fortnight, perhaps longer, you will see the same master in charge of many hinds, but the day comes when he is no longer fit to hold them. He will be " run out," as they say in the deer forests; a very tired monarch, with belly tucked up, a shadow of his former self. And, inevitably, a younger beast, fresh from the hill, will challenge him and topple him.

A rutted-out stag retires to recuperate. He may join up with several others in like case, and the group will graze and sleep in company, regaining their strength, and perhaps attended by a knobber. The stags have to get into some kind of condition to face the winter, which is why an early winter, with snow and frost, following close on the rut, takes such toll of weakened beasts.

Fights become common now among other stags carving up the harems, or trying to take complete possession. Night after night their roaring echoes in the glens. Most of the activity takes place from nightfall onwards, though stags roar on and off throughout the daylight.

With red stags, fighting is rarely a serious or bloody affair. Most fights are arguments, with the weaker beast quitting early on. There is much threat and

bluster, certainly, and the stags parade before each other in awe-inspiring fashion. But there is rarely serious fighting, and little damage to either.

Sometimes, of course, one stag does kill another. Some are wounded slightly. Very infrequently, two well-antlered stags will get their antlers locked. But mostly the rut is full of sound and fury, and very little more, although it is important to the deer.

Hummels, though hornless, often collect the biggest harems. And a switch stag, with his great rapiers of antlers, is more often than not a master. Hinds don't choose the stag with the bonniest head; the strongest stag takes possession and the hinds show little interest one way or the other.

With the rut over, stags and hinds form into their own herds, though you will always find the camp-followers of the opposite sex with some groups, on and off during the remainder of the winter.

In the old days, when we had the wolf, the wolves harried the deer, and controlled their numbers, as they still do in other parts of the world. Nowadays, since adult deer have no real predators in this country, man has to do the controlling. Whether he does so well or indifferently, or does so at all, does not concern us here. Nor does sport, which is frequently confused with, and identified with, control.

Red deer are found outside the Scottish Highlands in several parts of Britain —notably Exmoor, the mountains of the north of England, and in Ireland. But Scotland has, by far, the bulk of the red deer in Britain.

In Scotland deer are stalked with a rifle. In the south of England they are hunted by the Devon and Somerset staghounds. In Scotland there are too many deer, and deer where they should not be, but there is no kind of deer policy, and poaching by brutal methods is rife.

In the Highlands stags are stalked from August into the rutting season. Hinds are killed in winter, usually from November to January, but only certain beasts are taken. Milk hinds, suckling calves, are not killed. The beasts wanted are yeld hinds, which are hinds without a calf at foot, and therefore in prime condition. In night poaching, all kinds of beasts are shamefully slaughtered.

Red deer feed mainly in the morning and evening, but in the Scottish Highlands, where they are little disturbed for most of the year, they will graze during the day. They spend much of the daylight lying on the high ridges, even in midwinter, moving down to the glens late in the afternoon to grass and water.

Their sight is very good; their sense of smell acute and highly selective even at long range. You may fool a deer by sitting perfectly still, even when you are exposed to view, but you will never fool a deer's nose if the merest whiff of you is carried on the wind. Yet they are curious, and you can play on their curiosity so

57

long as you are not recognisable and provided that the wind is in your favour.

No beast is more sensitive to weather changes, and a herd will move before a storm breaks, coming down to seek cover in woodland or sheltered corrie. Storms will bring them down; fair weather sees them trekking up the hill again. Even in savage winter weather, they will lie by day on the ridges if the sun comes out and the wind dies away. In the course of twenty-four hours they may move up and down 2,000 feet or more.

Their movements in winter may be no more than a descent from the high ground to the lower slopes and the glens, but many deer travel long distances to their winter range.

Red deer of both sexes wallow in peat hags, but wallowing is most frequent in autumn when flies are troublesome. Stags wallow a great deal during the rut, when they rise from the peat holes, dripping glaur and water, like legendary monsters. In very hot weather you will see the deer, hinds and stags in velvet, on the highest ground, congregating where the wind keeps away the flies.

The red deer is our biggest land animal, stags standing over three and a half feet at the withers. Hinds are smaller. Weight varies a great deal, park deer coming heaviest as you would expect.

Wild red deer, anywhere, will eat anything that takes their fancy, and where they have access to agricultural areas they can cause a lot of damage to crops. Even in summer they will raid cornfields; in winter they will break into potato pits. Stags are usually most guilty, and one stag soon collects company, so that damage can be serious. In woodland, they can do some damage to young timber by stripping the bark. They are untidy browsers, and rip off twigs about six feet from the ground.

Grass is, of course, the main food, and deer can take the most coarse and unpalatable kinds. That is not to say they don't like the other kind, which they will graze if they can get to it. They will take hay put out for sheep or ponies.

Like the roe deer, the red species can eat yew without ill effect. All kinds of vegetation are eaten, including heather, ivy and the produce of orchard or garden. Barries of many kinds are eaten in the autumn.

Red deer vary a great deal in appearance, the coat coming in all shades from light brown to near-black. White beasts appear now and again, like the milk-white hind of Loch Treig, who was never fired at, and who was supposed to have lived for a hundred and sixty years in the wilds of Lochaber. More likely she lived for fewer than twenty years, with many generations of her descendants, born white, helping to create the great legend. One could almost wish such stories true.

But the old Gaelic legend: thrice the age of a horse the age of a man; thrice the age of a man the age of a stag—cannot stand up to the remorseless research of modern times.   At twelve, the Highland stag is in his prime, and probably, by then, he has lived two-thirds of his life.   Perhaps four-fifths of it. . . .

CALVES: *Born June. Spotted for about 8 weeks.*
RUT: *September/October. Some years into November.*
STAGS: *Cast antlers in spring. New antlers September.*
TAIL: *Visible—about six inches long.*
SIZE: *Stags 3½ to 4 feet at withers. Hinds smaller.*
WALLOW: *Both sexes wallow. Stags especially during rut. In May, when casting winter hair, wallows used frequently, and hair found there.*
YELD HIND: *Hind with no calf at foot.*
HUMMEL: *Stag which never grows antlers.*

Fallow Deer

FALLOW deer are found over most of England, but less commonly in Scotland as a whole. In some places, notably Perthshire, Ross-shire and Argyll, there have been wild fallow for a very long time, probably for close on two centuries in the area of Dunkeld and Blair Atholl. They are of much greater antiquity in England, where they were brought, according to tradition, by the Romans.

It is now believed by most people that the fallow deer of to-day are the descendants of animals imported from southern Europe, although we had fallow in prehistoric times. Wild fallow have lived in Epping Forest for many centuries.

We usually think of the fallow deer as a park deer, an ornamental species, and certainly most deer parks have them, while the neighbourhood will hold deer which have escaped from the parks. But wild fallow we have, in both England and Scotland.

Much bigger than our native roe deer, the fallow is several inches shorter than the red, but a good southern buck will weigh as much as many a poor Highland red stag. As with other species, the fallow doe is a smaller animal than the male. She is hornless.

Small herds are the rule with wild fallow, much smaller than in the red deer, and the sexes mix from before the rut until the spring. The rut is in October and November. At this season the bucks wallow; they challenge and fight. But they are not noisy. Bucks snort during the rut, but can also bark like the does. Both doe and fawn bleat. But, generally speaking, this species isn't notably vocal.

There are two distinct colour types in the fallow deer. One, which might be called the normal, is reddish fawn with white spots in summer and grey-brown, unspotted, in winter. The dark type is without spots in summer, and very dark brown. Both types occur in wild herds, as well as in deer parks.

The antlers of the fallow buck are palmated, which means they flatten out on top. They are notched along the back edge.

Fallow feed on much the same food as the red deer, and are especially fond of acorns, chestnuts and beech-mast. I believe, like the roe, they like mushrooms. This species sometimes strips the bark from hardwood trees at the " pole " stage.

The fallow likes plenty of cover, and the truly wild ones are shy and secretive. When they are feeding in the open they usually keep on the move. They panic readily, and when put on foot appear to run without either plan or leader.

Old fallow bucks tend to be most nocturnal in habit. They also tend to keep by themselves even during the period of herding.

(There are several species of foreign deer now free in certain parts of Britain —notably the Sika—but there is no space to discuss them here.)

SIZE: *Buck: 3 feet 2 inches; weight under 200 pounds.*
                  Does: Smaller.
FAWNS: *Born May and June. Spotted.*
RUT: *October. Duration short.*

Roe Deer

WE ARE in the habit of speaking of roe as woodland deer, as though our other species were not. But this needs some qualification. . . .

Where there are roe and woods you will find the roe in the woods, some of them most of the time and some of them some of the time. You will also find them in other places, even near towns.

Roe deer will be found in young plantations, mixed woods, mature forest where there is some cover, bracken thickets, gorse brakes, birch swamps and rushy hollows. In the Highlands, you will quite often find them on the hill, living the spartan life of the red deer.

Many Highland roe spend much of the year—even the greater part of the year—on the open hill. In winter, or during bad weather, they will seek tree cover, but in summer and good weather they haunt the ridges and slopes.

I have found the fawns of the roe on the open hill, at varying heights, right up to where the eagle nests. So you see it isn't easy, or advisable, to lay down the law about what kind of ground roe may frequent.

The beasts do, however, have strong likes and dislikes. They like leafy shade in summer, and dense woodland in winter. Marshy ground, well watered, attracts them. Birch swamps are a favourite haunt. They like open grassy clearings in woodland. Highland roe, during the heat of summer, will often lie out on the high ridges, where the air is cool and the flies scarce.

In my own area, the roe spend much of the summer in birch thickets and open woodland. Some of them stay out in the heather. In winter they seek out the thickest cover to shelter in, and at all times they like to be handy to open areas of grass and other forage.

The male roe is known as the buck—never a stag. The female is called the doe. Young roe may be called either fawns or kids, but never calves.

A mature roe-buck will stand something over two feet at the shoulder; he may measure only 2 feet 1 inch, or up to nearly 2 feet 6 inches in the biggest specimens, but animals of the latter size are most exceptional. Does are smaller than bucks, and kids of a few days old are little bigger than hares.

As a rule, only the bucks grow antlers, but once in a while a doe will be

found wearing them. Why some does should be thus attired is not known. It is generally thought that a horned doe cannot breed, but this is incorrect. I have seen a horned doe nursing twins, less than a mile from my house.

The antlers of a fully-grown roe-buck are in the region of nine inches long, and six-point heads—three tines to each antler—are normal. Bucks will be found carrying more points than that, and all sorts of malformed heads turn up from time to time; but six-point heads, measuring nine inches or less, are common.

Weight, length, and texture of antlers vary widely from place to place, and even on the same ground. I have two, taken from the same wood, indicative of this: one is $10\frac{1}{2}$ inches, heavily pearled, the other is $8\frac{3}{4}$ inches and poorly pearled. The larger is twice the weight of the smaller.

Roe-bucks, like red stags and other deer, grow new antlers each year. In the case of the roe the bucks cast their old antlers in November, or thereabouts, and their new ones are fully grown and clean from March onwards. Casting may be late, as cleaning may be, and some bucks will be found with antlers still in velvet well into April.

In buck fawns, the first growth of antlers does not follow the adult pattern. In late autumn two protuberances appear, which are very obvious by November. On these grow the first antler buds, or "buttons," which are rubbed off about February. Then the first real antler spikes begin to grow and these may be cleaned any time during May or June.

First proper heads (that is, in the young roe's second summer) are often a single spike, of varying length, or a spike showing signs of a fork. It is the habit to say the young buck grows a single spike in his second summer, two points in his third and three points in his fourth, but this sequence tends to vary a great deal from place to place and between individuals in the same place. It is, however, broadly speaking, a fairly general rule.

Roe antlers, like those of other deer, are covered in velvet during the growing stage, and it is when he is rubbing this off—cleaning or fraying are the terms used—that he does some damage to young trees. Young trees, against which a buck has been fraying, are scuffed and burred up to two feet from the ground, the stem and the underside of the low branches receiving attention. There is much unrealistic talk about the economic importance of such damage.

Cleaning time is not the only time that bucks rub, and thrash with their antlers. They do so during the rut, which is understandable, and at other times without apparent reason. I have watched a buck thrash goat willow, fireweed and low-spreading branches of elm. Any down-pointing branch that looks remotely like antlers is liable to be attacked playfully at any time.

During the rut the bucks often fight fiercely, and I have watched two fight a running battle along the edge of one wood (300 yards), across two fields (another 400 yards) and into another wood where I lost sight of them. I have seen one buck throw and stab another in flank, and I have watched two young bucks attack an old one. But, though the fighting can be fierce enough, and quite bloody in some cases, deaths must be extremely rare. A beast takes so much, then gives up before he is seriously damaged. Deaths, I imagine, must be accidental, and I have seen only one.

At this time the bucks can be unpredictable and temperamental, or, as I have heard it described, they " become cheeky ". I watched one buck assault and rout a fox, and another which attacked a collie and killed it. The dog had nineteen stab wounds on its body. During the period of the rut I have seen a buck chase hens, a pheasant, sheep and calves, presumably because his blood was hot and he had to be chasing something.

Because roe have no close season, does are frequently shot when they have young fawns. The motherless youngsters are either killed by natural enemies, like foxes, or they die of starvation. Exceptionally, one may be found, and adopted, by another roe doe—or a human being. But people who rear bucks should be careful, because a grown buck who has lost his fear of man can be dangerous.

Except in certain circumstances, roe deer are not great movers, and I am sure that many beasts spend their entire lives within a couple of miles of a given place. Bucks often, but not invariably, leave the does for a spell after the rut, rejoining them some time in October. During this period they may wander quite a bit, but the real stravaiging is done by single bucks after they have cleaned their antlers, and such beasts will stray right out of their own district.

By and large, however, roe are stay-at-homes, though they make considerable seasonal movements within their two-mile radius, or whatever their home range may be.

Fawns are born in late May and early June, any time after 23rd May in my own area. But out of season fawns can be found. I watched fawns being born on 4th July; there are records later than that, and earlier than 23rd May, from other parts of the country.

Twins, in my experience, are usual. Single fawns are common, though I often wonder how many of them are real singles and not the survivors from twins. Triplets are rare, but seem to be more common in certain areas. I have seen several families of triplets near home over a period of many years.

The summer coat, or pelage, of the roe is foxy-red; in winter it is usually grey. The winter coat is shed in the spring, sometimes as late as the end of May or early June. I have seen a doe with fawns when she was still casting hair. The winter coat is grown in October. The fawns are spotted at birth, but the spots disappear in August (later if the fawns are late-born) and the youngsters become like the adults in appearance.

In winter roe are clannish, though groups are not often large. Brian Vesey-Fitzgerald has seen twenty-five on the move in Hampshire, which must be exceptional. I have seen seven regularly, in a tight unit, and eleven in loose company, all on their home ground.

The winter groups cling pretty much together until the bucks are due to clean. From then on the young bucks tend to wander, and the old ones to keep to themselves. The does retire to give birth to their young in May and June, after which they are rejoined by the bucks. Then the rut takes place, followed by the buck's temporary absence from the family. On his return the winter group forms again.

A usual group in late autumn is buck, doe, two fawns, and one or two yearlings. It may only be buck, doe and fawns of the year; it may be larger. A buck with doe and fawns is devoted to his family in the sense that he is prepared to fight for them.

I have had a buck barking at me and stamping his foot when I was looking at his doe's tiny fawns. I have had one face me in winter, barking and grunting, fronting for his doe and family. And I had the unique experience, in the winter of 1946–47 of seeing a buck, with his herd at his back, threatening no fewer than four foxes who were harrying the deer in the deep snow.

Roe do quite well even in the hardest winters so long as they have woods and hedgerows. Any roe I have found dead in winter have had full paunches; they didn't die of starvation. Indeed, the heaviest mortality among roe has been, in my experience, in the month of May, when full paunches were the order of the day.

Roe take a wide variety of food. Fawns, when still very small, begin nibbling tender leaves and shoots, especially hawthorn. After weaning, they eat as adults.

Evening and morning are the roe's main feeding times, but in quiet places, and on the hill, they will graze on and off during the day. They are browsers as well as grazers.

Among other things I have seen them eat grass, hay, clover, docks, snakeweed and brooklime; the leaves and twigs of many hardwood trees, many kinds of berries, but especially doghips; the leaves of the raspberry and bramble; mushrooms, chat potatoes, turnips—even yew and a small piece of fish from a bird table. They will eat a variety of garden plants, including wallflowers and roses, and, in severe winters, they may punish young larch trees.

At night, and when feeding, roe are often quite vocal. Their bark is gruff, dog-like and far-carrying. I have had a buck barking at me when I was watching at a badger den at midnight. They can also grunt like hogs. Does have a special call for their fawns (like *whee-yoo*) and the fawns *peep* in reply. A frightened fawn screams like a child.

For their size, roe are great jumpers, and a full grown animal will clear six feet. Fawns will get under fences by crawling on their bellies. A fawn a month old can clear over two feet, which indicates that roe of any age can jump almost three times their own height.

In this country, man and his dogs are the grown deer's only enemies, if one forgets the fox. Foxes prey on fawns when they can; a single fox can handle a wounded yearling; two foxes, or more, hunting together can pull down an adult which is sickly, severely wounded, or wasting.

Two things about the roe are worth special mention. In the matter of breeding there is the phenomenon known as delayed implantation, the result being that, though roe mate in July/August, there is no obvious development of the young until the end of the year.

The other point is the habit of ringing. During the rut the bucks chase the does in rings—single rings, or double rings joined to form a figure of eight. Not all roe do this, although running in circles is a habit with them all. Used rings are well worn, and are visited each morning. They are often called fairy rings.

It is much easier to watch roe during the mating season if you can find yourself a set of these rings.

FAWNS: *Born May/June. Spotted till autumn.*
RUT: *July/August.*
BUCKS: *Cast antlers November. New antlers April.*
RINGS: *Usually round some object—tree, bush or boulder. Sometimes, rarely, in standing corn.*
SIZE: *2 feet 1 inch for bucks. Does smaller.*
MARKS: *Rump buff in summer; white in winter.*
TAIL: *No visible tail. Doe may have hair-tuft in winter.*

The Brown Hare

TRADITIONALLY, hares go mad in March, which is another way of saying that March is their mating season, for then they buck, and jump, and kick, and caper all over the fields. But they go slightly mad at other times of the year as well.

However, the main period of madness—what you might call the peak period—is in spring; from February to April. Scottish hares start boxing and chasing each other a little later than English ones, and there may be little activity until well on in March, or even early April. Usually they are capering about the time the rooks are cawing in the rookeries. Thereafter they have their little tournaments, on and off, until late in the year, for hares breed several times in a season.

It isn't difficult to watch them at this time, for they aren't at all secretive about their displays. A big buck (or jack) will career all over the place, chasing does and fighting with other bucks, and you can watch a gathering of seven to fifteen, or even more hares in a field in broad daylight. I've seen nearly twenty in a field in Perthshire close by a main road, and have watched a group of seven to ten for two hours at a time, over several days, at home.

The bucks—they are smaller than the does by the way—leap up, forward and sideways; they chase each other; they kick and they bite. You'll find a strong buck holding a clear space round his doe of the moment, fighting off any other hare that comes in. You'll see him chasing other hares, while the doe may crouch flat or sit up watching. When the buck approaches her she may accept him, or she may fight him off. Quite often, the does give the bucks some hefty kicks.

Young hares, called leverets, are born from March onwards as a rule, but I've known a doe give birth in February, when there was snow on the ground. I've seen newly born leverets in late September, and you'll find them much later than that. A family of leverets may number up to five. Three or four are common, and there are records of six and even eight. Four is the commonest family in my part of the country.

Unlike young rabbits, leverets are born above-ground, furred, with their eyes open, and able to run about. They have wavy, silky fur, redder than that of old hares, flecked and freckled with silvery-white or pale buff.

Despite their social gatherings hares are, for most of the year, solitary beasts, and this trait is noticeable from the beginning of their lives. The hare's nest, or form, is a simple couch in the open, sheltered by nothing more than a tussock or a clump of rushes. Soon after the birth of her young, the doe carries each one in her mouth to a little form of its own. And in these the leverets stay, until called out by the doe at feeding time. Then they will suckle her, and perhaps play around her for a short spell; afterwards each returns to its own form.

Some hares, however, have their nursery form in a wood, in a gorse brake or in deep heather. As a matter of fact, quite a number of hares spend a lot of their time in woods, where they'll lie up during the day. They move out into the open to feed in the evening. In severe weather many hares move into woods for the day, and I put them on foot repeatedly with my dogs.

When the doe hare moves her leverets to separate forms, she may not be aware of the wisdom of her action, but wise it certainly is. Such tiny creatures, crouching in the open, may be found by a prowler or trodden upon by the hooves of cattle or sheep. If they are in separate forms the risk is lessened; one may die but the others may be missed. But, in my experience, leverets are trampled very rarely indeed by grazing animals. A leveret so trampled, and injured, is usually left to its fate.

The mother keeps careful watch on her young family, and I have watched does driving cattle and sheep off when they approached too close to the leverets' forms. At this time, a doe has a great deal of real courage, and will assault a stoat if need be, kicking the prowler with her big hind-feet. At other times, a stoat can send her bounding away in terror.

When returning to her leverets to nurse them, the doe breaks her trail by taking great sideways leaps. This means that any nose which takes up her line will find several breaks to slow it down or defeat it. I saw a wonderful example of this when there was snow on the ground. The hare had her leverets under a tree, and her tracks showed three tremendous sideways leaps to break her line. They showed also two such leaps when she was leaving them.

When the hare is very small, its enemies include the fox, stoat, cat, hawk, owl and dogs. Once it is past the half-way stage, it is beyond the power of hawks and owls, and most cats. When fully grown its enemies are man, dogs, foxes, stoats and exceptional cats. In the north, it has other enemies: the golden eagle and the wildcat. But the hare usually taken by wildcat and eagle is the blue, or mountain, species.

Against these natural enemies the hare has her speed, her endurance and her cunning. She has, when hunted, as many tricks as the fox, and is an adept at running back on her own line then leaping sideways. A hunted hare prefers to run uphill. When overtaken she twists and turns sharply, so that her pursuer loses yards before being able to change direction.

A strong hare can run a sheep collie into the ground. By her sudden twists she can often give a greyhound best. But it takes a strong and clever hare to escape an experienced greyhound if the dog is within thirty yards when she is put on foot.

She has her favourite exits from, and entrances to, her home fields, the gate she likes to pass under, the break in the wall she likes to leap through. So she is easily ambushed, netted and snared. Because her eyes are placed far back on her head she can see well behind her, but not so well in front. In her form she will lie facing the wind, relying on her eyes to watch where she can't smell. Yet men who know the hare can outwit her and pick her out of her form.

Hares do not stick to one form all the time. They have several, chosen to suit different weather conditions, for the hare likes shelter and a view. In winter a hare will sometimes lie up in a snowdrift which is often the most comfortable place of all. Hares do not burrow.

The hare shares with the rabbit the habit of refection, which means that all food passing from the bowel is re-swallowed and passed through the stomach again.

Mountain Hare

THE mountain hare is a whimsical, unpredictable beast, here to-day and gone to-morrow, sensing the coming of a storm and shifting ground before it breaks, moving from the heights to the glens or from one side of a mountain to the other.

I remember driving one evening over Schiehallion in Perthshire. The light was fading fast, and we gave up all hope of reaching the stalker's cottage before nightfall.   Then the snow began to fall, swirling against the windscreen, so that it was difficult to see ahead even with the headlamps full on.

The snow came down in great, goose-feather flakes, playing tricks with our eyes in the headlight glare.   When the first white shape crossed the road ahead we thought it was some witchery of the floodlit snow-dance.   But it was a white hare.

They began to cross in fives, sixes and dozens, some hopping, others running; white, spectral shapes flitting silently through the headlamp beams before vanishing in the swirling snow.   That night there was a raging blizzard and by morning the hills were white as far as eye could see.

Like the red deer, the mountain hare is weather-wise.   But it doesn't always take a storm to make them move out.   An eagle can clear a hillside temporarily. But storms and eagles apart, the hares will shift ground suddenly, in a body, without apparent reason.

Compared with the brown hare the mountain hare is smaller, shorter in the ears and legs, and not so heavily whiskered.   His coat is far more woolly and the black tips to his ears are not so striking.   In winter he changes to white; this change is complete in the mountains but not always so on the islands.   Because of his change of coat and the ground he lives on, he is known as the mountain hare, the blue hare, the white hare, the snow hare and the varying hare.

The mountain hare breeds probably twice a year, and has smaller families as a rule than the brown hare.   They are born in the open, among stones or boulders, or even under cover of heather or a peat bank.   Unlike the brown hare, the mountain species will go to ground readily, in peat banks or among rocks, and seeks this kind of cover when there is an eagle scouting overhead.

Its main enemies, when adult, are the eagle, fox and wildcat, as well as man and his dogs.   Leverets are killed by buzzards, ravens and crows as well, and the peregrine falcon will take them at times.

Mountain hares, when lying up, are often reluctant to move, so that they can be killed with sticks or even picked up by hand.   At other times they are as wild as wild goats.   Sometimes they become very numerous in certain places, and drives are organised to kill them down on sheep ground. They are not difficult to herd, and staggering bags used to be made in a day on the hill.

Their food is heather, grass and other mountain vegetation, and they can exist on a hard diet of rushes, moss and lichens.

When hard weather drives the hares down to cultivation level you may then see them on the brown hare's ground, and sometimes there is interbreeding.   The poorest beasts are the first to come down.   Here and there the ranges of brown and blue hare overlap, but in the main they keep to their own territories, the blue on the high ground and the brown on the low.

74

The Rabbit

UNTIL the disease called Myxomatosis killed off ninety-eight out of every hundred rabbits in Britain, we had the beast so long with us, and it was so familiar to everyone, that we had ceased to think of it as an alien. But an alien it is. It is not one of our native animals.

The rabbits which you used to count in hundreds in the fields can now be numbered in twos, and people have been wondering if the disappearance of the rabbit will not upset the balance of nature. But what about the upset to the balance of nature when the rabbit was introduced to this country? The upset began then, when the presence of rabbits meant an increase in the food supply of many hunting animals.

It seems probable that the Normans brought the rabbit to Britain, where it was at first confined in " warrens," the name now given to the burrow system of any rabbit colony. In time it spread over England, and into Scotland, but it was not until the nineteenth century that it colonised the Scottish mainland as a whole.

Because it was a sporting animal—treated as game in fact though it was never game in law—and provided cheap meat and fur for felt hats, it was never treated as vermin as it should have been. It was introduced to Australia with appalling consequences, with which we are all familiar. Are we as familiar with its costly and destructive habits in our own country?

For many reasons the rabbit has had, and always will have, its supporters, usually those people who do not have to feed it. Myxomatosis has dealt the species a heavy blow, but we still have the rabbit. And it looks as though we shall go on having it. Many isolated colonies were not touched by disease; they are still there. And in areas almost cleared by disease, the rabbit is making a come-back.

In this country the disease spread in two main ways, through the rabbit's own flea, and by human agency. It was made an offence for human beings to spread the disease, but this could have no effect on the final result. And Myxomatosis, by the way, was not something created in a laboratory by some devilish scientist; it is a rabbit disease prevalent in certain parts of South America.

To-day we can speak and write of the rabbit, in most places, as a scarce animal. Though I now see rabbits daily, there are still more hares than rabbits on the

ground round about me. I am sure we have as many foxes as rabbits on that ground. But what about this year and next? Rabbits can multiply at high speed compared with foxes.

We always looked upon the rabbit as a burrower, and it was. Most rabbits lived in holes in the earth or among rocks, but there were always those beasts which lay out in the open: outliers we called them. The rabbits I am seeing now appear to be all outliers. They are also much more shy by day than rabbits used to be. And they are breeding successfully because I am seeing young ones in all stages of growth.

Young rabbits can be seen, and nests found, in almost any month of the year, but the main breeding season appears to be from January on to late summer. The young may be born in nests in the main warren, or in separate short burrows called " stops," close by or some distance away. I often find such stops in woods, banks and hedgebottoms, 200 yards and more from the nearest colony.

The doe makes her nest of grass and other material, mixed and lined with wool plucked from her own body. This is placed at the end of the stop, which is usually about the length of a man's arm, though often deeper. The young, when born, are blind and naked. The doe closes the stop after nursing her young, and seals the entrance with earth, but this earth eventually shows traces of rabbit wool mixed with it, thus betraying the stop to human eyes.

At this stage, the young rabbits may be found and killed by fox, badger, stoat, hedgehog or rat. I have found a hedgehog asleep in a stop, completely gorged. The doe visits her young only to nurse them, then, at the age of about three weeks, they come outside and may be seen with her grazing. Once they are completely weaned they are left to fend for themselves. They may stay on in their stop, and enlarge it into a proper burrow, or they may join up with the nearest colony. Young rabbits which stay on in their nesting burrow are the founders of new colonies.

Where rabbits burrow in river banks they are often flooded out, and many drowned. But the burrows are never empty for long. Survivors, and others, move in, and they never seem to learn the dangers of water, for year after year the same burrows, liable to flooding, are occupied.

Sometimes a doe rabbit will construct her nest above-ground. I have found several such nests, built into the heart of a rush clump or similar place, and I remember one, which contained five naked young, which was placed on the ground under a gorse bush.

Rabbits feed late in the day and in the early morning, but where they are not being disturbed they will graze on and off during the day. They do not like heavy rain, but they will feed during a light fall of snow. When the ground is covered with snow, they will scrape holes in it to get down to grass. During a period of snow they are more liable to attack the bark of trees, and often do a great deal of damage to young plantations. The Forestry Commission has to spend large sums every year netting plantations against them.

Despite its enemies, and the fact that many young ones never reach the stage of being born (they die in the early stages of development), rabbits were legion before Myxomatosis almost wiped them out. Fox, badger, wildcat, stoat, otter, pine marten, polecat, weasel, hedgehog, rat, dog and cat—not to mention birds like the eagle, buzzard, raven, crow, owl, kestrel and magpie—killed rabbits according to the size they could handle, yet the beast's staggering reproduction rate kept it well ahead of them all. And ahead of man with his guns, traps, dogs, nets, snares and gas.

Lots of people miss the sight of a colony of rabbits moving out, in waves, from a wood to a field in the evening, but it is a good thing to look at the field to-day and remember what it used to be like. To-day the corn grows right to the wood-edge. In the old days it would be eaten down, right along the woodside, and for twenty yards out. No grain was harvested from that close-cropped area.

You should make a point of reading a book called *The Rabbit* (by Harry Thompson and Alastair Worden) which is the best ever done on the subject and likely to remain so for many years to come.

Brown Rat

O N THE 18th of November, 1953, there was a big rat hunched on a shelf in my meal store. My wife mistook it for a hedgehog. The rat squealed at me and leaped among bags of grain, in which defensive position it managed to bite my terrier twice before she killed it.

That brown rat measured one foot six and a half inches long, and weighed 1 pound 12 ounces. A pound and three quarters is a big rat, but not as big as the monster mentioned by Wentworth Day, which was killed by the rat-catcher Willie Dalton. It measured two feet two inches long, and weighed two pounds six ounces.

These, of course, were big rats, and one was a very big rat indeed. Rats have long tails, so long beasts are common enough, in the order of sixteen inches or so; and they will weigh, mostly, up to a pound. But rats much longer than that, longer than the one my terrier killed, are far from uncommon. The weight is the thing, and that varies from under a pound to nearly two pounds.

The brown rat came to Britain in ships from Europe, where it had arrived from Asia. It reached England early in the eighteenth century, and George I has been blamed (by Jacobites) for bringing it; it reached Scotland around the time of the '45 Rising. The older black rat (mistakenly called English) reached England before Bannockburn, but was probably not settled in Scotland until the sixteenth century. Anyway, both species are aliens.

The Old English black rat was pushed out of most of the countryside by the vigorous, colonising brown species, which can live almost anywhere including sewers.

In cities, towns and villages—in farms, warehouses and shops—on mountains, islands and on the shore—in all such places the brown rat can thrive and multiply. In recent years, spectacular results have been obtained in rat destruction by the use of certain baits, but the rat we still have with us.

Country rats, which infest farms, farm buildings and stackyards, move out in strength for the summer, and take up residence in rabbit burrows, water vole burrows, walls, banks and coups. In the buildings they can be poisoned easily; when they are spread over the countryside this becomes impossible. The out-living summer rat provides the new legions.

Though rats are prolific breeders, and you will find a female nursing young when she is carrying another litter, females do not produce families continuously through the year. My terrier has killed many females which were neither nursing nor carrying young. But breeding goes on throughout the year. My terrier has dug out a nest of eleven in midwinter, after a badger had already tried; I was able to help the terrier by breaking through the frozen sand with a pick.

When I was in my farmhouse I used to allow a few rats to live in peace in the empty stable so that I could watch them. I would put down oats on a tray and watch them scurrying out from their holes, picking up the oats and racing back into their holes again. I used to put out hen eggs for them, but have never yet seen one rat lying on its back, clasping the egg, while another rat pulled the carrier away. I have, however, met people who say they have seen such a thing. All my rats rolled the eggs away under their chins, and heaved them up over obstacles with their forepaws.

They will, however, use their tails to get water which they can't reach directly. They dip the tail then lick it, as a cat will put its paw in a milk bottle and lick it.

Rats are extremely courageous, and resourceful; they are also very wary and intelligent. But they are also creatures of habit. It has long been known that a rat will continue to go round an obstacle when the obstacle is no longer there! I tried this many times with obstacles in my stable. Once the beasts were running round it, I removed it. They continued for a whole night, and sometimes for a second night, to run round the place where it had been.

The courage of the beast is beyond question. A cornered rat, or a wounded rat, will face a terrier or a fox. It will face a man, squealing like a pig, and will attack a man in the open if it has no hole it can run to. I have a film of my son having a fight with a rat in a field. It leaped at him, biting his gloved hands, and hanging on to the seat of his trousers! I have watched an inexperienced terrier dancing in circles with a big rat swinging by the teeth to her jaw.

Rats destroy food at all stages from growth onwards, and do vast damage in the country. They will also kill anything they can catch and hold. They kill rabbits in the nest. They kill small birds. They take eggs, and can even manage to remove them from under a sitting hen!

Many poultrymen consider the rat their main, perhaps their only, enemy. One spring I had a batch of chicks under an infra-red lamp. Chicks were disappearing every day. Then I found my big cat curled up under the lamp one morning and blamed him, though he had never touched a chick in his life. I decided to watch him, and catch him in the act. I watched him, and he killed a rat! The rat was the culprit and the cat had been waiting for it.

Summer rats will climb high to birds' nests. I have seen one in an ivied tree after the eggs of a woodpigeon, and several raiding blackbirds' nests in the ivy growing over a wall.

Though they do have many enemies, rats have been greatly helped over the years by gamekeepers who destroy all those enemies as a routine. High on the list of rat-killers come the weasel and the fox; but there are also the stoat, the eagle, the buzzard, cats, dogs, owls and hawks. Birds like the kestrel and the owls take small rats. The eagle will take them any size at all. I photographed a long-eared owl eight times in a night when he came to the nest with eight rats! They were small rats, but they were still rats.

The rat has always been a spreader of diseases. The old black rat helped the Great Plague along. The brown is also a carrier of plague; it carries several diseases of livestock; and it causes a serious disease in people, especially coal miners, when they eat food contaminated by rat urine. The bite of the rat may be little to look at—compared with, say the bite of an otter or badger—but it is highly dangerous because of possible infection.

Apart from disease, the menace of the rat is probably best illustrated by the example of North Rona. On that remote island the people died of famine because the rats had eaten their entire store of winter food. It is a grim story, made no less grim by the fact that the rats themselves died off because they could not survive without the people.

The Mole

THE mole—the little gentleman in black velvet, to use a Jacobite description—is more often seen dead than alive, which isn't surprising in the case of an animal who spends practically the whole of his life underground.

Moles may be turned out by the plough, or dug up with a spade; they may be howked up by foxes or chased out by weasels. I once watched a kestrel pull a wriggling mole from the heap in which he had been working; she killed him, with difficulty, but didn't carry him off. All these can be classed as involuntary appearances! But moles do come above-ground of their own free will.

I can recall seeing many moles on the surface, going about their business of the moment—two males fighting in a leafy hollow, with one killing the other; a mole killing a woodmouse (and eating it) in a dry ditch below a bank; a male chasing a female up and down a wheel-rut; a mole emerging from a tunnel to drink in a narrow ditch. All these incidents took place very early or late in the day.

When the mole is on the surface he can travel at an amazing speed. His pace has been described as clumsy. I would not call it that. A man has sometimes to go faster than walking pace to keep up with a mole on hard ground, and I have a film which shows this. I can't believe that even the mole could make such speed underground, although it has been said that he can. He can dig himself out of sight in less than thirty seconds, but I doubt if he could travel through earth at anything like his ground speed.

Early spring is the likeliest time to come on a mole above-ground. Then, if there are two moles, they will either be males fighting or a male pursuing a female. I imagine they must be more sociable underground judging by the fact that a number can be taken in the same tunnel.

Moles may tunnel down to water, or send a tunnel into the side of a ditch. They will break through the grass roof of their tunnel to take a worm, and may even come right out to pick up worms after rain, as I once saw a mole do.

Good times to see live moles are during spring and autumn ploughing. If you follow the plough a mole will sooner or later be turned up. This is the way I have collected my captive moles. And captive moles can tell you a great deal.

You'll discover that the mole's appetite is prodigious; that you have, so to

speak, to go out and work for him. Depending on worm-size, he will eat a worm every twenty minutes right round the clock. If he has no food for six or eight hours he becomes a weak, wasting mole; twelve hours starvation, or less, will kill him. He likes lots of water to drink. Fortunately, he will eat a lot of things besides worms; more fortunate still some of the patented cat foods suit him very well. That saves you working like a mole yourself.

A captive mole will eat mice, frogs and lizards, attacking them with unbelievable savagery. He will eat wireworms and leatherjackets. But he won't take vegetable food. All these things apply, I imagine, to moles in the wild state.

When the mole finds earthworms in abundance he will store a supply for future use. The queen wasp paralyses caterpillars with her sting; the mole paralyses worms with a bite. Dead worms wouldn't keep fresh; live ones do. It was a naturalist called Adams who first proved this habit of the mole by giving captive animals more worms than they needed. They bit the surplus worms and buried

84

them. In my garden frame I found such a worm store. I have never seen a second one.

Owls and kestrels will not, in my experience, eat a mole. Nor will fox, stoat or weasel. I have had cats which caught moles, but none which ate them. I have found dead moles from time to time at a fox den, but they were used as playthings by the cubs. The velvet bodies became dried and mummified but were never eaten.

No animal is better adapted to the kind of life it leads than the mole. He has a barrel-body, a sharp face, hand-like forefeet, tiny eyes well-buried in fur, and a coat which stands on end so that it can't be rubbed the wrong way. When burrowing, he bores with his head and scrapes with his forefeet; then he turns and pushes the loose earth along to his last " shaft ". This earth, when pushed above-ground by the mole, forms the well-known heaps you see all over the place.

The nesting heap is a different affair altogether. For one thing it is much bigger, a foot or more in height and a yard across. The nest of grass and leaves is in the middle, with galleries leading from it. In this the young moles are born in April and early May, sometimes later. By July the young ones are self-supporting. Very young moles have been found later than July, but most are born a couple of months before.

You will find such big heaps, containing nests but no young, and these are simply sleeping quarters. Male moles have their own nests, also built in such fortresses. Galleries lead to and from all fortresses, but there is no special plan or pattern. It is a simple matter to section one of these heaps with a sharp spade in autumn, and you will see for yourself.

Winter nests are often in huge heaps, and are used year after year. As many as seven nests have been found in a heap, one on top of the other. I have seen four and three, and have found a mole dead in one in February.

There is a rough, wet, rushy pasture near my home—it is, indeed, in the middle of a moor—where I spend much time studying kestrels, owls and other birds. Moles swarm on this ground, and here I have seen a nest in a rush tussock, completely above-ground. On this ground moles surface quite frequently early in the morning, as I have seen when I was in a tree hide waiting for kestrels.

Moles swim well, and high in the water, with the tail well up. I watched one in a deep peat ditch swimming for nearly a hundred yards without much effort. I don't know whether it had fallen into the ditch by accident, or was swimming because it wanted to. Perhaps it was trying to drown its fleas!

Quite often, when I see a mole-heap heaving in a quiet spot, indicating a mole at work, I stand by just in case. It is surprising how often the mole will poke his head out, especially early and late in the day. The most likely place to see this (it doesn't always happen, though) is at a heap where the mole has just begun work.

Mice, Voles and Shrews

TO MOST of us, all the little mouse-like beasts are mice. But they are not all mice. Some of them, the shrews, belong to the same family as the hedgehog and the mole. Mice, on the other hand, are rodents, which puts them in the same family as the rats, squirrels and rabbits.

The wood-mouse is often called the long-tailed field-mouse, while the name short-tailed field-mouse is used for the field-vole. Shrews are often called shrew-mice. In my part of the country the children use the name screw-mice. Since mice and voles belong to the rat family, you would expect any big mouse or vole to be called a rat; this, in fact, happens with the water-vole, which is nearly always called water-rat.

By and large, people are probably most familiar with the house mouse. Many colour varieties of this species are bred in captivity and kept as pets. It is not a native of this country. And it cannot live without man. The house mouse of St. Kilda, which had its own special features, died out when the island was evacuated.

This is the mouse which swarms in corn stacks, riddling them with tunnels and making meal of the grain. Many house mice, in the country, live out in the fields in summer, moving into houses and stacks for the winter. In towns, they live indoors most of the time.

House mice live almost entirely on food provided by man. They will carry away surplus food and store it. The males fight each other and the females fight for mouse-holes. The nest is domed, and made of straw, paper, rags, or anything soft that is handy. Though usually shy, these mice can become very bold where they are not being molested, and will come out in bright light when there are people about. A cat in the house makes them far more wary.

House mice will eat almost anything, and cheese is the favourite bait for traps. They steal, and ruin, much grain. They will eat insect food.

The long-tailed field-mouse, or wood-mouse, is a handsome little animal, with big ears, pinky-white feet, and a tail as long as its body. The fur is some shade of brown, but there is much variation; the under parts are silvery-white and clearly lined off from the brown, or yellowish, fur of the flanks. On the chest there is very often a bright patch coloured orange or pale red.

87

Field-mice are very common almost everywhere, from the low ground to the mountain tops. They are mainly nocturnal, but many must move by day judging by the number killed by kestrels. Owls kill them at night. The field-mouse's enemies are legion: cats, dogs, stoats, weasels, foxes, crows, ravens, rooks—even moles. But the field-mouse manages to remain our most common animal.

I have found field-mice nesting in a stackyard, but I have rarely come across one in a stack of corn. Periodically, one finds its way indoors, but this is exceptional. The nest may be above-ground, in a warm tussock, or underground in a burrow with several entrances. The nest is made of grass, and the burrow is most often in a bank under a hedge or in standing crops. Many mice are turned up by the plough in autumn.

The field-mouse does not hibernate. Like the squirrel it is active throughout the winter in suitable weather. It gathers food—grain, haws, acorns and such like— and stores it, quite often in the old nests of thrush or blackbird. It is very destructive in the garden, and will take peas, bulbs, other seed, and fruit.

There are many " races " of field-mice in this country, most of them on islands, but they are for the specialist. In the south of England, however, there is a big field-mouse called the yellow-necked mouse, having a yellow collar as the name suggests. But even about this one there is some doubt, for it interbreeds freely with other field-mice and may be no more than a variety.

The tiny harvest-mouse—tawny above and white below—weighs only a quarter of an ounce. It is not a common animal, is becoming rarer, but is most plentiful in the south of England. It is also found in small numbers in the southern counties of Scotland.

This mouse frequents cornfields, where it is active by day, climbing up the stalks of oats, wheat and barley. It curls its tail round the stalks. It will eat the grain on the stalk, or nibble off the ears so that they fall to the ground to be eaten there. It eats seeds other than grain, and tender shoots and leaves. Like so many of the tiny ones, the harvest-mouse can become cannibal in captivity.

The nest of the harvest-mouse is built about a foot from the ground, woven round the stalks of corn or other strong plants, and sometimes in a bush. Here the young are born. Nests used in winter are often under corn stacks, but burrows are also used in the open fields, and there the animals store food. Harvest-mice do not hibernate, but are less active in winter. In summer they are sociable and playful.

We have three species of vole: the water-vole, field-vole, and bank-vole. By far the biggest is the water-vole, often called water-rat. The other two, as in the case of the mice, have many varieties found on a number of islands, but at this stage they needn't concern you.

The field-vole is very common, blunt-faced with a short tail; it is the one called the short-tailed field-mouse. In some years it reaches " plague " numbers, with thousands taking the place of hundreds, and at such times they can do enormous damage to young plantations and pastures. Some years ago there was such a plague not far from my home. The grass yellowed; vast numbers of young trees were damaged or destroyed; a whole flock of short-eared owls moved in to breed and prey on the voles.

Despite the presence of owls, kestrels, weasels, foxes and others—all cramming themselves with vole meat—a plague runs its course. Then the voles die off suddenly, till only normal numbers are left. This sudden drop is called a " crash " by zoologists, but what causes it to take place nobody yet understands very clearly.

Voles are burrowers, making their nests at the bottom of a hole about two feet deep, but they also have a system of runways, or creeps, in the grass. These radiate for considerable distances, and are actually hidden by the grass roof which

the voles leave as cover. Despite this system, however, large numbers of voles are killed by owls, kestrels, foxes and others.

The field-vole is active by day and night. It does not hibernate. Occasionally, odd-coloured field-voles are found. I have seen a white and a cream.

The bank-vole is smaller in the body, and a little longer in the tail, than the field-vole, and it is more mouse-like. It is also far more active and agile, and will bite when handled. If you want to keep hold of a bank-vole you need a very deep box, for it is a great jumper; it can leap out of a milk bottle or a box nine inches deep.

Bank-voles are not so common as field-voles, but are found in most parts of the country, becoming rarer in the north and north-west of Scotland. This species likes banks covered with ivy and other trailing growth, and under such cover it has its runs. It will use mole runs. In banks it has its burrows, and in these it has its sleeping quarters.

The water-vole is a very dark-furred animal, blunter in the face than the brown rat, more robustly built, and often killed because it is mistaken for a rat. Its size makes this mistake understandable, for a good specimen of a water-vole will measure 15 inches over-all, a third of which will be tail. Adults vary in body length from under 7 to about 10 inches.

The brown rat is, in fact, an enemy of this vole. It will invade the burrows, and live in them in summer. And it swims very well. So the water-vole suffers both ways; he is attacked by rats and attacked by man who mistakes him for a rat.

Water-voles are clannish animals, and live in small communities. The burrows are often extensive affairs, with entrances and exits above and below water. Sometimes they are at a distance from water. The nest is made of chewed reeds, or other water-plants, and may be in a burrow away from the water. Water-voles have a habit, the reason for which is not understood, of carrying underground green stalks which are not used for food or bedding. Two litters are reared by many females, and there may be a third.

In the north of Scotland water-voles are often quite black in colour, and all are darker than animals from the south. I have seen very handsome glossy specimens which country people looked upon as a cross between a mole and a water-vole.

The water-vole, when alarmed, dives with a distinct plop; sometimes, when he is surfacing, he brings up a screen of water plants with him. He is active by day from spring to autumn, and you will find him nibbling willow shoots or the grass along the bank of a stream. In this country he does no damage. He is preyed upon by owls, stoats, weasels, rats, dogs and cats. He does not hibernate.

Shrews are kinsmen of the moles, eating the same kind of food in the same enormous quantities. In appearance they are very like mice; but you can tell them by their long, pointed snouts.

The common shrew is found all over Scotland and England but is absent from the main islands and Ireland. It is a miniature tiger, fighting with other shrews, mice and voles. It can kill and eat mice. Its life is one continuous search for food. If deprived of food for a few hours it will die.

It has a strong musky smell, as you'll find if you keep a couple in the house. This musk smell has been called a protection; it isn't. It saves the animal from being eaten, but doesn't prevent it from being killed. Cats, dogs, foxes, stoats, weasels, owls and kestrels kill them, but, of these, only the kestrel and the owl will eat them. It may well be that a hunter will kill shrews when it is well fed and has nothing better to do, but when hunting for food it may avoid them because it has no time to waste and already knows that they are useless as food.

The common shrew doesn't burrow much; it prefers to use the runs of voles and the tunnels made by mice. Its nest, which is of dry grass, will be found under cover of some kind, or in a hole in a tree. More than one litter is reared in a season,

but there is very high mortality in autumn, as you must have noticed. It is almost certain that the shrew's life does not exceed 18 months.

The water-shrew is a dark-furred species (with white belly) which frequents the same places as the water-vole. It drives smaller burrows into the banks of streams, and has entrances above and below water. It dives well, and finds its insect food by turning over stones on the stream bed. This species is seldom found far from water.

Kingfishers are said to eat them. I know that owls kill and eat them, because I have recorded several brought to nests.

The water-shrew, like the common species, will kill and eat anything it can catch and hold, including its own kind. The usual food is insects and their larvæ, spawn, small fry, worms, snails and slugs.

Smallest of the shrews is the pygmy, which weighs one-fifth of an ounce or less. It is the only species found in Ireland. It has been found on the top of Ben Nevis.

There is a fourth species of shrew which is confined to the Scilly Isles. It is small like the pygmy, but has white, instead of red-tipped, teeth.

The Hedgehog

THE hedgehog is familiar enough, if only as a prickly ball in a field or ditch. The ball heaves gently to the rhythm of breathing; it rolls easily if turned over by stick or foot; there is a chink in the armour where the beast's feet meet his snout.

Balling-up is the hedgehog's defensive action; the dense array of quills is his defence against would-be attackers. When you come on him at first he will lower his head, and crouch; approach a little closer and his brow quills will come down like a visor; come right up to him and he at once becomes a ball. The quilled ball is more than a hedgehog-defence. It is also a shock absorber when the beast tumbles, as he frequently does when climbing.

Effective as the hedgehog's defence can be, it is far from being proof against all comers. He has no chance against a man with a stick. His quills don't help him when he gets caught in trap or snare, and he finds his way frequently into both. I have taken the same hedgehog from a snare three times in one night! In the days of the horse he had nothing to worry about on the roads; to-day his kind are regularly killed by motor vehicles.

His wild animal foes are few—only two really—but they are deadly. They are the fox and the badger. If you add certain terriers that makes three serious enemies. The old writers—the ones with the old " vermin " outlook—used to say that if you had foxes and badgers about you wouldn't have hedgehogs. This is utterly untrue, and quite demonstrably so. At home I have them all.

The badger's way with hedgehogs is direct and ruthless: he tears them apart with his great bear-claws. Then he eats the prey down to the quilled jacket. My own badgers, given a hedgehog newly killed by a car, left only the barbed skin. I have seen such skins periodically—the result of a badger's work—but badgers are no more likely to exterminate local hedgehogs than eagles are to exterminate grouse. Nature was not such a fool as to make it possible for hunters to destroy their food supply and eat themselves out of existence. We have had badger and hedgehog in this country since time immemorial.

Though a killer of hedgehogs, the fox isn't in the badger's class. What I do know is this: a fox will try to drown a hedgehog, and I have seen one push a hedgehog into deep water then retrieve it when it was dead.

Most dogs will bark themselves silly when they find a hedgehog, but certain terriers can open them. I should think, however, that, as hedgehog killers, dogs take second place to foxes—after the badger.

The hedgehog is insectivorous, which means no more than that he has the right kind of teeth and does eat insects. It doesn't mean that he eats nothing else. More accurately, he could be called omnivorous, for he will take anything he can catch and hold. He will eat eggs, birds, mice, young rabbits, carrion, fish and the scrapings of the frying-pan. In captivity he will eat bread and milk, chocolates, sugar. And, of course, all hedgehogs like frogs.

It has been said that the hedgehog tears frogs limb from limb, and many may do so. But the animals I have watched simply began eating where they had a hold and carried on from there. I have seen them beginning at the hind-foot. And I have watched them starting their meal without bothering to kill the frog first.

I don't know whether hedgehogs swim for the sake of swimming, but they do swim well and buoyantly when they have to. Any hedgehogs I have actually seen swimming voluntarily were after frogs, and I have photographed one doing this. If you duck a hedgehog you will usually see a lot of fleas floating out from him, and I often wonder if the beast ever takes to the water for this purpose.

There is a pond near my home which I have visited regularly since I was a very small boy, seeking sticklebacks, frog spawn, newts and other things. Several times, in the spring, I have watched a hedgehog there catching frogs ashore or in the shallows. And it was there I saw some of them swimming.

A hedgehog which comes on a rabbit nest will kill the tiny young, and he may lie up there until he has eaten the lot. After rain, when the worms come up, you will find him on the lawn catching them. If you follow a hunting hedgehog—and it isn't difficult—you will see him weaving about, nosing in the tussocks, and you will hear the crunch of his teeth when he eats beetles and such food. He will eat any dead mouse he finds, and I have seen one making a meal from a snared rabbit.

Hedgehogs are true hibernators, and during the winter sleep they lose heat and are as near death as it is possible for a living animal to get without actually dying. The pulse slows down. The breathing is hardly noticeable. Warmth will wake them up. But one can't lay down hard and fast rules about the duration of the winter sleep.

For example, I have seen a hedgehog on Christmas Day. I haven't seen any (except dead ones) between then and the middle of March. But the hedgehog is often bedded down in November; he may not wake until early April. I suppose weather and temperature have much to do with this. Zoologists tell us that a special gland plays a part in the hibernation habit of the hedgehog, and we already know that all of them lay on a lot of fat, which is used up during the sleep. Recent

95

work has also shown that the sugar content of the animal's blood falls greatly at the time of hibernation.

When the hedgehog wakes up he is often a bit woolly-headed, and liable to fall asleep again for a day or two. I have found one fast asleep with an earthworm coiled round his snout. The hedgehog was only partly coiled.

There is probably much to be said for the belief that hedgehogs mate for life, but considering the high death rate on roads life isn't very long for many individuals. Mating takes place in spring, and young hedgehogs are born in May and June. Many females have a second family in August or later, and you will sometimes see such a family about late in September, in daylight (after sunrise or before sunset). Newly-awakened hedgehogs, like those preparing for sleep, are quite often out during the day.

The quills of baby hedgehogs are soft and almost white. They don't harden, or turn dark, for about three weeks. Before the quills harden the young hedgehog is an easy prey for species which couldn't tackle an adult, and I can name a cat I knew and a carrion crow as examples. I fancy any flesh-eating animal would take baby hedgehog, just as many people will eat adults!

I wonder how many snakes hedgehogs kill? They can, and do, kill them. Curiously, though, I have offered adders to a lot of hedgehogs without ever witnessing an attack by the hedgehog on the snake. In confinement, the adder was always the more ready to attack, the hedgehog merely squatting, nose to ground, while the snake lashed itself against his quills.